D1204371

DATE DUE	
DEC 1 6 2000	DEC 0 1 2003
FEB 0 7 2001	
MAR 2 3 2001	FEB 0 7 2004
SEP 2 2 2001	
DEC 2 2 2001	FEB 0 1 2005
JAN 2 9 2002	FEB 1 5 2005
	JAN 1 8 2006
FEB 2 7 2002	MAR 2 9 2006
MAR 0 8 2002	
DEC 1 7 2002	
FEB 2 6 2003	

ST. JOHN THE BAPTIST PARISH LIBRARY
1334 WEST AIRLINE HIGHWAY
LaPLACE, LOUISIANA 70068

COMUS

FRENCH OPERA HOUSE

FEBRUARY 27th 1900

MARDI GRAS TREASURES

INVITATIONS OF THE GOLDEN AGE

COMUS

IMAGE COMUS 2005

MARDI GRAS TREASURES

INVITATIONS OF THE GOLDEN AGE

Henri Schindler

PELICAN PUBLISHING COMPANY

Gretna 2000

ST. JOHN THE BAPTIST PARISH LIBRARY
1334 WEST AIRLINE HIGHWAY
LaPLACE, LOUISIANA 70068

Copyright © 2000
By Henri Schindler
All rights reserved

This book is dedicated to Jon Newlin.

The word "Pelican" and the depiction of a pelican are trademarks
of Pelican Publishing Company, Inc., and are registered
in the U.S. Patent and Trademark Office.

Library of Congress Cataloging-in-Publication Data

Schindler, Henri.
  Mardi Gras treasures: invitations of the Golden Age / by Henri Schindler.
    p. cm.
  Includes index.
  ISBN 1-56554-722-5 (hc : alk. paper)
   1. Invitation cards—Louisiana—New Orleans—Catalogs. 2. Invitation
cards—Louisiana—New Orleans—Design. 3. Carnival—Louisiana—New Orleans—History.
I. Title.

NC1880 .S36 2000
394.2'5'0976335075—dc21

00-039150

Page 1: *Gentleman's admit card to the first Mistick Krewe of Comus Ball, 1857.*
Page 2: *Invitation to the Mistick Krewe of Comus Ball, 1890: "The Palingenesis of The Mistick Krewe."*
Page 3: *Detail of invitation to the Mistick Krewe of Comus Ball, 1906: "The Masque of Comus." Design by Jennie Wilde.*
Page 5: *Gentleman's admit card to the Krewe of Proteus Ball, 1890: "Elfland."*
Page 6: *Invitation to the Mistick Krewe of Comus Ball, 1881: "Myths of Northland." Design by Charles Briton.*

Printed in Hong Kong
Published by Pelican Publishing Company, Inc.
1000 Burmaster Street, Gretna, Louisiana 70053

CONTENTS

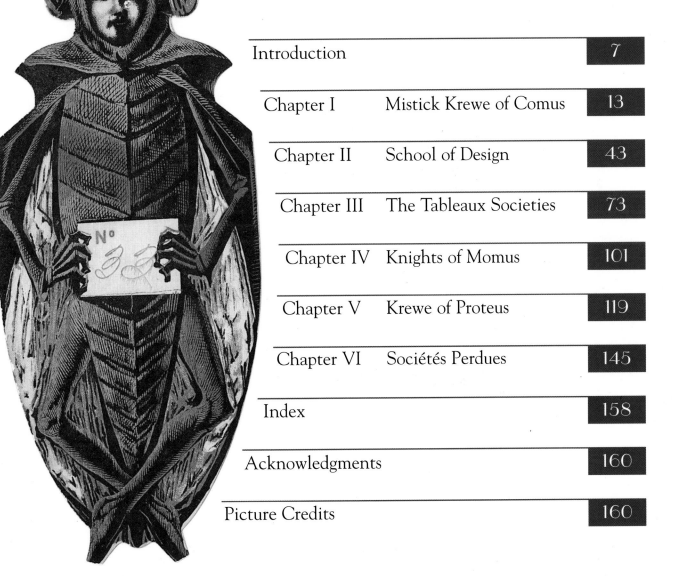

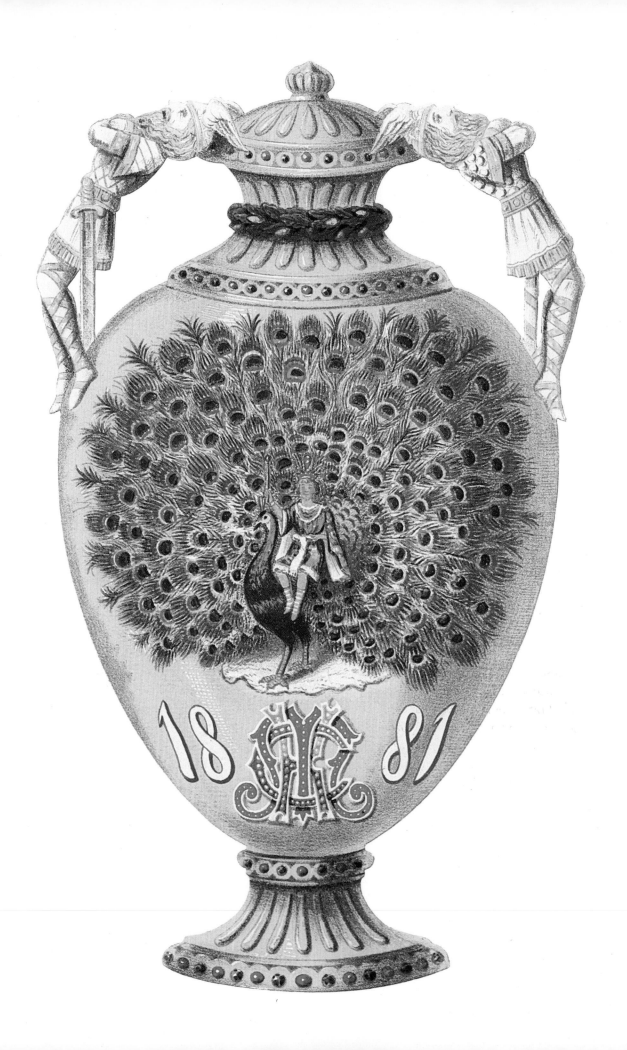

INTRODUCTION

The fantastic empire of New Orleans Carnival returns to life every winter, with its festive panoply of masquerades, balls, feasts, and pageantry. New Orleans is never more herself than during this reign of folly and ritual calendar of earthly delights—when the deities of forgotten pantheons and the splendors of long-vanished courts are restored for a season, summoned into being from the gilded vaults of the old city's memory.

The celebration of Mardi Gras and its evolution into a near religion have been the subject of several histories, among them Perry Young's magisterial *The Mistick Krewe* and this writer's *Mardi Gras: New Orleans*. It is impossible to describe even one Mardi Gras, as Young lamented in *Carnival and Mardi Gras in New Orleans*:

> "Carnival subsists like epiphytes on atmosphere—on whispers, exaggerations, pretensions, on shams, secrets, imagination and make-believe, on paint and pictures, on artlessness and art, on gauds and glitters, on buffonery, on beauty—enemies of language that make the loftiest adjectives run pale."

But if the spirit of Mardi Gras eternally defies description, each season deposits some fragments of its brilliance. This book is the first of four volumes devoted to the presentation of those fragments, the fantastic hoard of decorative art and design created during the Golden Age of Carnival. With the documentation of these treasures—the ball invitations, fabulous floats, costumes, and jewelry—we hope to illustrate the indelible resonance of Mardi Gras in the psyche and culture of New Orleans.

The early Creole population of New Orleans, descendants of French and Spanish colonial settlers, created an urban culture and sensibility that was unique in North America. New Orleans was Latin and Catholic, and still burnished with allegiance to the throne and love of pomp. Travelers and writers of the early 1800s were mesmerized by the sub-tropical city, with its quaint architecture, narrow streets, and exotic vegetation; they marveled at the exuberant diversity of races and languages in the public markets and squares; and they noted the curious cemeteries lined with avenues of tombs. Above all, visitors and diarists were dazzled by the Creole zest for living, and the Creole passions for music and dance.

The first public ballroom, *La Salle Condé,* opened in 1792, and by 1840 the city enjoyed eighty locales for dancing. There was music everywhere in New Orleans: in the ballrooms and theaters, in public squares and in the streets—seven days a week. (Puritan visitors were ashen with concern, particularly about performances violating the Sabbath.)

Indeed, music was an early New Orleans export. The city's two opera companies toured the country, and composer Louis Moreau Gottschalk rose to international prominence with his piano performances of Creole melodies and the Bamboula dances of Congo Square.

The Protestant, Anglo-Saxon Americans residing in New Orleans offered a stark contrast in temperament and culture to the old Creole society, and a mutual disregard existed for generations. With the Louisiana Purchase in 1803, New Orleans ceased her existence as a French colony, and reluctantly became, in name, American territory. With the coming of the first steamboat in 1812, nearly a century after its founding, the city's wealth and greatness blossomed. New Orleans became one of the world's fabled ports, famous for its pursuit of pleasure, its love for music and dance, and its Carnival.

Nineteenth-century New Orleans, like Venice, was a city in love with magnificence and masks, with baroque spectacles of theater and pageantry—with Carnival, which always began on Twelfth Night, the feast of Epiphany, climaxed with Mardi Gras, and ended with the arrival of Ash Wednesday. On Mardi Gras, maskers of every description marched and danced through the streets of the old Creole sector, and when night fell there were numerous masquerade balls open to anyone with the price of admission. But not all of the festivities were public. There were private soirées in homes, as well as subscription balls staged by the elite in the city's numerous theaters. Creole society later moved their grandest entertainments, which often lasted until daylight, to the princely St. Louis Hotel. One was invited to these balls or one did not attend. Louis Fitzgerald Tasitro, an Irish actor and writer visiting in 1841, was there:

"Towards ten o'clock the whole troupe [of maskers] marched off to the Bal Costume at the St. Louis Hotel; and the picturesqueness of their appearance—the infinite variety and multitude of their costumes gave an air of grandeur which is difficult to imagine. I was sorry to see so many Anglo-Americans in their customary black and blue colors—black trousers, blue coats, and nameless hats. But even they, cold emblems of the marble age, could not dim the splendour and magnificence of the magic scene. Besides the Bal Masque at the St. Louis there were at least nine or ten 'soirees dansantes' in different quarters of the city . . . in fact New Orleans was one vast and gallopading hall. . . . People seemed to have nothing else to do but to amuse themselves—to drown their senses in forgetfulness—to make their Saturnalia as long as possible."

No physical scintilla of those revels exists—there is no shred of silk or scrap of gaily colored paper that can be linked to the boisterous antics or opulent balls of the 1830s and 1840s. Completed in 1842, in the American sector, and proclaimed one of the largest and finest in the world, the first St. Charles Hotel was a grandiose testament not only to the economic and political ascendancy of the Anglo-Americans, but to their version of New Orleans style. In 1851, the palatial building was burned to the ground in three hours. From its ashes rose the second magnificent St. Charles, and it was to the frescoed, gold-leafed ballroom of that hotel, also destroyed by fire long ago, that guests were summoned to a *"Soirée Dansante"* on a January evening of 1854—with the oldest extant invitation to a New Orleans Carnival ball.

Three years later, on Mardi Gras night, the Mistick Krewe of Comus made its legendary debut with the first torch lit procession and the first thematic floats ever seen in New Orleans. Between them marched a host of demons and devils, cavorting in the glare of torches to the music of brass bands, and dressed in fabulous costumes and wearing masks of papier-mâché, impersonating "The Demon Actors in Milton's *Paradise Lost.*"

The historic procession was followed by the inaugural Comus ball, with another Mardi Gras innovation—the Krewe alone was masked; their guests, the Anglo-American elite of Louisiana, were not costumed for a masquerade—they were attired in the formal suits and fashionable gowns usually worn to the opera. The parquette of the Gaiety Theater had been raised to the level of the stage to accommodate the sparkling scenic tableaux of *"Paradise Lost"* and the dancing that would follow. There were four tableaux. The first presented "Tartarus," with Pluto and Proserpine, and the fates, furies, and gorgons; next came "The Expulsion," depicting Beelezebub, Moloch, Isis, Dagon, and Mammon. The third tableau, "The Conference of Satan and Beelzebub," presented Gluttony, Drunkenness, Indolence, Vanity, Discord, and Licentiousness, presided over by Satan, who was flanked by Sin and Death. The final scene unveiled "Pandemonium," the capital of Satan and his peers, and the curtain closed for an interlude. When the curtain was raised the stage had been cleared and at the back was raised a great arch of gas-jets, exclaiming in letters of fire: *"Vive la Danse!"*

Comus, in the course of a single evening, had re-created Mardi Gras. The scores of Carnival societies born during the next century all emulated, with varying degrees of success and eclat, the formats for parades and balls that were introduced by the Mistick Krewe. There is no visual record of that first triumphant procession, but a treasured handful of invitations and admit cards to the first Comus ball have survived. These early invitations are talismans of another age, an age that prized romance, literature, and the decorative arts. The earliest examples were elegantly printed combinations of motifs and symbols from the classical vocabulary of illustration, with masks, lyres, flutes, flowers, and ribbons; color was delicate, and sparingly employed.

The Golden Age of Carnival artistry began with the creation of new Carnival societies in the 1870s and early 1880s—Twelfth Night Revelers, Rex, Knights of Momus, Krewe of Proteus, and Phunny Phorty Phellows. Great wealth and inspired design marked the era's shimmering pageants and opulent balls; but while the grand processions were for all to see, the balls were private entertainments, and attendance was by invitation only. As many as four thousand invitations were issued to a Comus ball at the French Opera House, and a few thousand more to the Rex receptions at the Washington Artillery Hall. These invitations, together with admit and dance cards, reflected the theme of each ball, with exalted subjects drawn from mythology, history, epic literature, whimsy, and nature.

Technical advances in color printing and lithography also shaped the creation of these paper treasures. During the 1880s and 1890s, they grew ever more elaborate, employing die-cut layers of scenes that unfolded into fantastically detailed miniature tableaux. These beautiful summonses of the gods and kings of Carnival were not entrusted to the postal system, but delivered by special couriers.

Presented here are two hundred examples of the finest ball invitations and dance cards, masterworks of design and lithography, most of them reproduced for the first time. This catalog is far from complete: only one side of these cards could be shown; some of the larger ones are represented only by details; and there were dozens of painful omissions. The works are organized by krewe and presented chronologically; designers are identified when known. It is one aim of this series to attribute as much of their work as possible to the forgotten artists and designers of Carnival, for their incredible body of work was anonymous. The great Mardi Gras pageants and balls were indeed the province and production of the krewes, and the phantasmagoria of those offerings—infused with strange opulence, mystery and beauty, the exotic and the occult—still glows in the collective unconscious of New Orleans.

MARDI GRAS TREASURES

INVITATIONS OF THE GOLDEN AGE

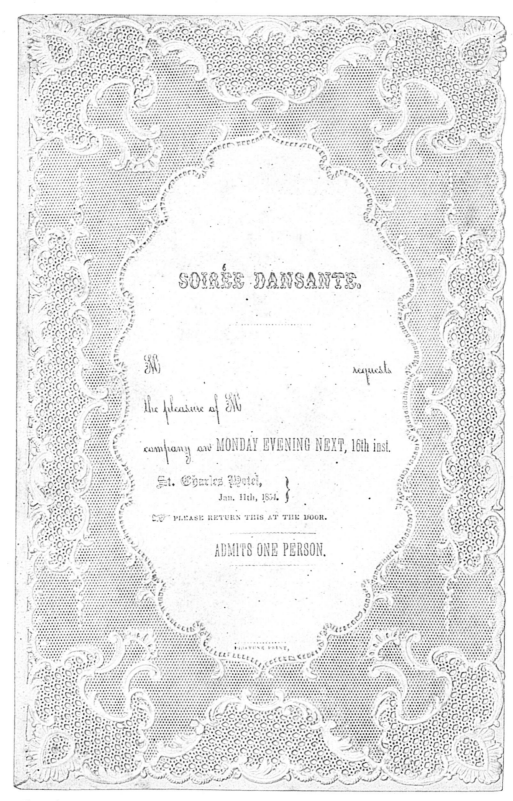

This 1854 invitation to a soirée dansante at the St. Charles Hotel, framed by an intricate border of delicately punched paper, is one of the earliest surviving Carnival invitations.

CHAPTER I

MISTICK KREWE OF COMUS

The starting point of most cosmologies is the triumph of order and form over chaos and confusion, and the beginning of a "Golden Age" of harmony and plenty. So this survey of Carnival gods and their earthly gifts begins, as they all must, with Comus. It was Comus who, in 1857, saved and transformed the dying flame of the old Creole Carnival with his enchanter's cup; it was Comus who introduced torchlit processions and thematic floats to Mardi Gras; and it was Comus who ritually closed, and still closes, the most cherished festivities of New Orleans with splendor and pomp.

The Mistick Krewe's fondness for literature and mythology were quickly established. John Milton's Comus was a sorcerer, the son of Bacchus and Circe, who offered his cup to quench the thirst of weary travelers lost in his wood; soon as they tasted, their bodies remained the same, but their heads were changed

> "Into some brutish form of wolf or bear,
> Or ounce, or tiger, hog or bearded goat,

> And they, so perfect is their misery,
> Not once perceive their foul disfigurement,
> But boast themselves more comely than before,
> And all their friends and native home forget,
> To roll with pleasure in a sensual sty."

Comus, whose hedonism was equaled only by his guile, spoke some of Milton's most seductive verse:

> "Meanwhile welcome joy and feast,
> Midnight shout and revelry,
> Tipsy dance and jollity.
> Braid your locks with rosy twine,
> Dropping odours, dropping wine.
> Rigor now is gone to bed,
> And advice with scrupulous head.
> Strict age and sour severity,
> With their grave saws in slumber lie.
> We that are of purer fire
> Imitate the starry quire. . . .
> By dimpled brook, and fountain brim,
> The wood-nymphs, decked with daisies trim,
> Their merry wakes and pastimes keep;
> What hath night to do with sleep?
> Come, let us our rites begin;
> 'Tis only daylight that makes sin."

For his second production, in 1858, Comus chose to illustrate "The Classic Pantheon" with thirty-one ornamental cars and floats, followed by a ball that featured four tableaux, "Minerva's Victory," "Flight of Time," "Bacchanalian Revel," and "Krewe Procession." The early invitations contained suggestions of that year's theme, as well as vignettes representing past productions; they were printed every year by a different lithographer, and while the quality was consistent, the designs seem almost pieced together with elements from stock printing catalogs.

The invitation for 1866 depicted the subjects "The Past, the Present, and the Future," and it marked the return of the Mistick Krewe to Mardi Gras following the Civil War. Scenes illustrating each of the first five years of Comus were brightly painted in a series of vignettes; the years devoured by the war, 1862 through 1865, were suggested in a haze of ashen gray. The name of Edward Arnold appears in the lower right corner of this invitation, one of the very few to be signed by the artist; Arnold, a native of Heilbronn, Wittemberg, and a respected marine painter active in New Orleans for twenty years, thus became our earliest known Carnival artist. There is no record that he was involved in any earlier Mardi Gras work, and little opportunity was to follow—Arnold died the following fall, on October 14, 1866.

The pre-war heights of prosperity were never again attained, but New Orleans remained the largest and wealthiest city in the South. The early 1870s brought the creation of three new Carnival organizations, Twelfth Night Revelers, Rex, and the Knights of Momus, whose parades and balls followed the methods and manners of Comus.

The old Creole sector continued to attract writers and artists, several of whom came to rank among the most important Carnival designers. The great Charles Briton, a Swede, came to New Orleans following his adventures in Mexico; he designed the floats and costumes for the principle pageants of the 1870s and early 1880s, and his hand can be seen in a number of invitations. For the Comus procession and ball of 1873, Briton designed the satiric masterpiece, "The Missing Links to Darwin's *Origin of Species*."

Invitations to this ball offered no suggestion of its ingenious theme, but the program was profusely illustrated with tableaux groupings of the Briton caricatures, which depicted members of the carpet-bag regime as all manner of strange creatures.

The pronounced influence of the Aesthetic Movement began to be seen in the Comus invitation and admit card for 1880, "The Aztec People and Their Conquest by Cortez." The mysterious Aztec symbols, the ripples of moonlight on a lily pond in Anahuac, and the stern visage of a boldly painted idol, all reflected the movement that turned for inspiration to the art and architecture of ancient Egypt, Greece, and Arabia, to what Lafcadio Hearn called, "the life of vanished cities and the pageantry of dead faiths."

The Comus Aztec invitation, curiously undated, was the Krewe's first to be printed on a weighty card stock, and the first to be saturated with the brilliant hues of the new chromolithography. Aesthetic motifs again appeared throughout the invitation for 1881 (the first Comus card to be die-cut), exploring another subject beloved by Hearn, and no doubt long familiar to Briton, "Myths of Northland." Comus was pictured on a golden urn, astride an enormous peacock.

The first visit of the King and Queen of the Carnival to the Court of Comus, a custom still honored today, took place at the Comus ball of 1882. It was somehow appropriate that this ritual closing of the Carnival season, in time, echoed the Comus theme of that year, "Worships of the World." Elaborate floral tributes decorated the proscenium box of the five young ladies honored at the Comus ball of 1884, daughters of Robert E. Lee, Jefferson Davis, Stonewall Jackson, and D. H. Hill. Comus himself took out Miss Mildred Lee for the first dance, and she is remembered today as the first Queen of Comus.

Following a six-year absence, during which he staged neither pageant nor ball, Comus returned in 1890 with his "Palingenesis," celebrating highlights of his remarkable history; the floats were designed by Bror Anders Wikstrom, one of the city's finest painters, but someone else—unknown—created the invitation. The year 1891 marked the debut of Virginia Wilkerson Wilde as the Comus designer, a partnership that lasted for two decades, earning acclaim for the young woman and new accolades for the Mistick Krewe.

Miss Jennie Wilde, as she was known throughout her career, was born on April 10, 1865, in Augusta, Georgia. Her grandfather, Richard Henry Wilde, was poet laureate of Georgia, and author of the popular "My Life is Like a Summer Rose." Wilde and her sister, Emily, lost both parents and their only brother (a writer and poet) when they were young girls. Jennie Wilde studied painting and antique drawing at the Art League of New York, and remained a member all her life. She also studied at the Southern Art Union, and her work was exhibited by the Art Association of New Orleans from 1889 through 1892. Like her father, grandfather, and brother, Jennie Wilde won a fleeting reputation for her poetry, but her remarkable designs for Comus—ball invitations, floats, costumes, and jewels—continue to charm and beguile the viewer.

In the year 1891, Wilde began her Carnival work with a masterpiece, the Comus invitation illustrating the theme, "Demonology." Guests to the Comus ball were summoned by a striking serpent, its green body of armor-like scales coiled and gleaming upon a card of bronze that, when opened, revealed a host of goblins, sprites, and demons being flayed by the devil. The Comus subject for 1892 was "Nippon, Land of the Rising Sun," a favorite theme of Aesthetic design that traveled effortlessly, as did Wilde, to Art Nouveau. (It should be noted that while the presence and influence of Lafcadio Hearn lingered long after his departure from New Orleans in 1888, in 1891 his brilliant work in Japan was only then beginning.)

Jennie Wilde became Carnival's high priestess of Art Nouveau. Her designs for invitations and dance cards of the late 1890s and early 1900s were animated with sensuous, flowing lines and dreamy vortexs, and adorned with delightfully inventive lettering and occasional cryptograms. Wilde frequently wove a design motif through every aspect of a given year's work, as in 1909's "Flights of Fancy." Comus greeted the multitudes upon a float of enormous papier-mâché pansies; his mounted aides carried riding crops decorated with metallic pansies set with rhinestones; and dance cards to the ball were purple die-cut pansies. The Comus invitations of this period were, with few exceptions, the only efforts of the old line krewes that continued to boast elaborate die-cuts and vivid lithography. With the dawn of the twentieth century, Rex and many others had begun to issue simpler engraved cards, emblems of their current modernity.

Jennie Wilde died in Measden, England, on September 11, 1913. The Comus subject for 1914 was "Chaucer," and while the float and costume designs were clearly Wilde's, the invitation bore no trace of her hand. In the following year, guests of Comus received engraved cards that were elegantly scripted and emblazoned with M. K. C., but this was visual confirmation, nonetheless, that one of the most dazzling collaborations in the history of Carnival had ended.

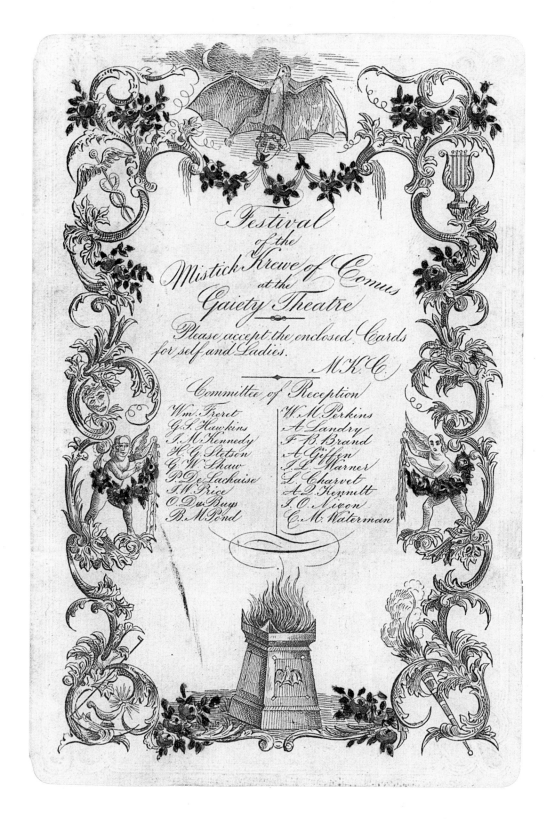

Festival
of the
Mistick Krewe of Comus
at the
Gaiety Theatre
Please accept the enclosed Cards
for self and Ladies.
M.K.C.

Committee of Reception

Wm. Freret   W. M. Perkins
G. S. Hawkins   A. Landry
T. M. Kennedy   F. B. Brand
H. G. Stetson   A. Giffen
G. W. Shaw   J. J. Warner
P. De Lachaise   L. Charvet
J. W. Price   A. J. Hennett
O. Du Buys   J. O. Nixon
B. M. Pond   C. M. Waterman

Above: *Invitation to the first Mistick Krewe of Comus Ball, 1857: "The Demon Actors in Milton's Paradise Lost."*

Opposite, above: *Invitation to the Mistick Krewe of Comus Ball, 1866: "The Past, The Present, and The Future." This was the first Comus ball after the Civil War, and the years 1862 through 1865 were painted in ashen vignettes. Design by Edward Arnold.*

Opposite, below: *Gentleman's admit card to the Mistick Krewe of Comus Ball, 1868: "The Departure of Lalla Rookh from Delphi."*

The legendary Comus pageant of 1873, "The Missing Links to Darwin's Origin of Species," was followed by the Krewe's ball at the Varieties Theater. This engraving from Scribner's magazine presents a scene from that Mardi Gras landmark evening; the fantastic papier-mâché rhinoceros was one of one hundred whimsical creatures presented in tableaux, beneath calcium lights and amid dissolving scenic views.

The final tableau of the Mistick Krewe of Comus Ball, 1873: "The Missing Links to Darwin's Origin of Species."

Dance card for the Mistick Krewe of Comus Ball, 1882: "Worships of the World." Design by Charles Briton.

Opposite, top: Invitation to the Mistick Krewe of Comus Ball, 1880: "The Aztec People and Their Conquest by Cortez." Design by Charles Briton.

Opposite, bottom: Lady's admit card to the Mistick Krewe of Comus Ball, 1880. Design by Charles Briton.

Invitation to the Mistick Krewe of Comus Ball, 1891: "Demonology." Design by Jennie Wilde.

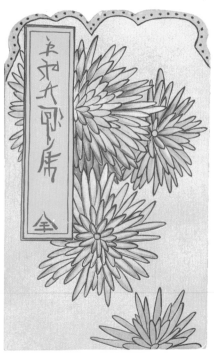

Above: *Invitation to the Mistick Krewe of Comus Ball, 1892: "Nippon, the Land of the Rising Sun." Design by Jennie Wilde.*

Left: *Detail, exterior panel, Comus invitation, 1892.*

Opposite, bottom: *Dance card for the Mistick Krewe of Comus Ball, 1891: "Demonology." Design by Jennie Wilde.*

Ye MISTICK KREWE of COMUS

Requests Your Presence at their Revelries, Shrove-Tuesday, February 18th 1896, at Eight o'clock French Opera House, NEW ORLEANS.

Invitation to the Mistick Krewe of Comus Ball, 1897: "Homer's Odyssey."
Design by Jennie Wilde.

Opposite, top: *Invitation to the Mistick Krewe of Comus Ball, 1896: "The*
Months and Seasons of the Year." Design by Jennie Wilde.

Opposite, bottom left: *Dance card for the Mistick Krewe of Comus Ball, 1896.*
Design by Jennie Wilde.

Opposite, bottom right: *Dance card for the Mistick Krewe of Comus Ball, 1897:*
"Homer's Odyssey."

Interior detail of invitation (above), dance card (below), *and exterior of invitation (opposite) for the Mistick Krewe of Comus Ball, 1898: "Scenes From Shakespeare." Designs by Jennie Wilde.*

Invitations (above and opposite, top) and dance card *(opposite, bottom)* for
the Mistick Krewe of Comus Ball, 1899: "Josephus." Designs by Jennie Wilde.

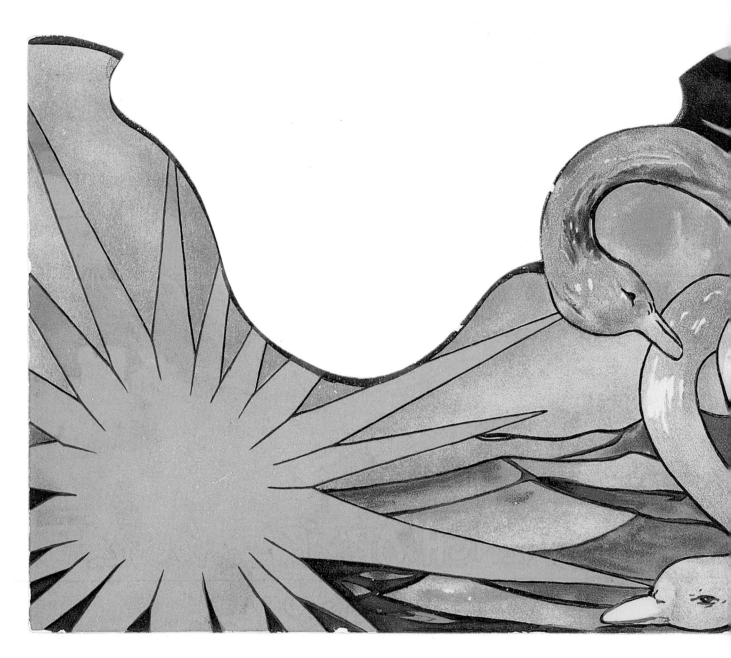

Invitation to the Mistick Krewe of Comus Ball, 1900: "Stories of the Golden Age." Design by Jennie Wilde.

Invitation to the Mistick Krewe of Comus Ball, 1901: "Selections From the Operas."
Design by Jennie Wilde.

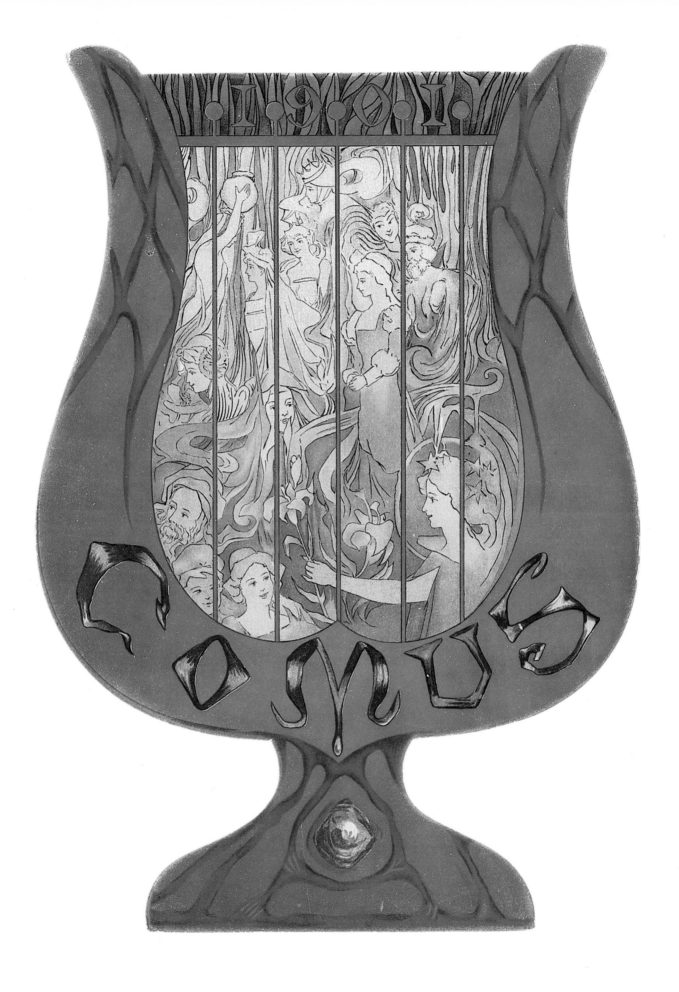

Invitation to the Mistick Krewe of Comus Ball, 1903: "A Leaf From the Mahabarata." Design by Jennie Wilde.

Top: *Dance card for the Mistick
Krewe of Comus Ball, 1904:
"Izdubar." Design by Jennie Wilde.*

Left: *Dance card for the Mistick Krewe of
Comus Ball, 1903: "A Leaf From the
Mahabarata." Design by Jennie Wilde.*

Detail picturing Ludlow Castle, where Milton's Comus was first performed in 1634—from the invitation to the "Golden Anniversary Ball" of the Mistick Krewe of Comus, 1906: "The Masque of Comus." Design by Jennie Wilde.

Opposite: Invitation to the Mistick Krewe of Comus Ball, 1905: "The Lost Pleaid." Design by Jennie Wilde.

Interior detail of invitation (above) and dance card (left) for the Mistick Krewe of Comus Ball, 1908: "Gods and Goddesses." Designs by Jennie Wilde.

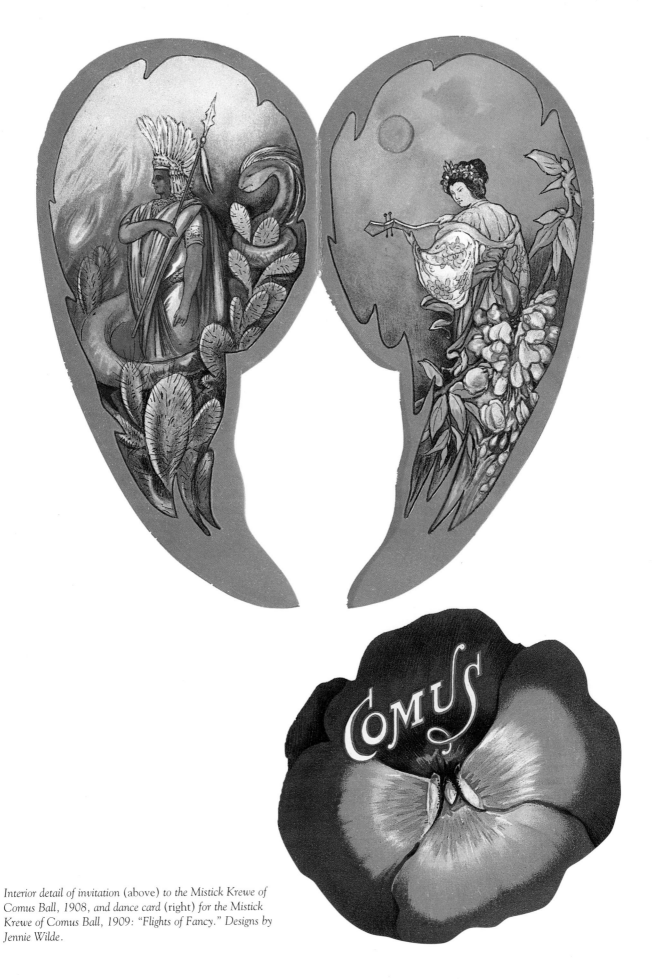

Interior detail of invitation (above) to the Mistick Krewe of Comus Ball, 1908, and dance card (right) for the Mistick Krewe of Comus Ball, 1909: "Flights of Fancy." Designs by Jennie Wilde.

Above: *Invitation to the Mistick Krewe of Comus Ball, 1925: "The Realms of Phantasy."*

Below: *Invitation to the Mistick Krewe of Comus Ball, 1931: "Jewels From Byron."*

CHAPTER II

SCHOOL OF DESIGN

In the closing days of the Carnival of 1871, an effort was made to revive the cavalcade and march of maskers that had been a fixture of the Creole Carnival years earlier. An anonymous call was posted for maskers to assemble and parade on Mardi Gras afternoon, but revelers did not respond. The following year an organization was hastily formed and its leadership pulled together a lengthy and festive procession of vans and carriages and maskers—all in honor of the visit to New Orleans of the Russian Grand Duke, Alexis Romanoff. While other cities had planned their welcomes for Alexis for months, New Orleans had done nothing. With only twelve days remaining before the royal visit, a group of businessmen, led by Edward C. Hancock, editor of the *New Orleans Times* and a key figure in Comus, decided to honor the Grand Duke with the Mardi Gras parade of a king—the first appearance of Rex, King of the Carnival.

Edicts and proclamations appeared daily in the press, signed "Rex" or "Bathurst, Lord High Chamberlain." Some of the orders, abolishing internal revenue collections, fixing a deliriously high market rate for cotton, and "dispersing that riotous body known as the Louisiana State Legislature," were amusing, bombastic fantasies that reflected the widespread discontent with the carpetbag regime. But many of the other decrees were seriously issued and obeyed: the closing of all city and private business; the interdiction of malicious mischief, and the cancellation of all quarrels, hatreds, jealousies, and vendettas; and the decoration of the city with banners and bunting of the royal colors—purple, green, and gold.

The 1872 procession was led by Rex riding a white bay charger and costumed in purple silk-velvet. His Majesty was followed by the milk-white *Boeuf Gras* (fatted ox), symbolizing the last meat to be eaten before the fasting of Lent. The mile-long cavalcade was filled with horsemen, gaily decorated carriages and wagons, and thousands of maskers, all interspersed with bands playing in march time the song that became the improbable anthem of Carnival, "If Ever I Cease to Love." ("May cows lay eggs and fish get legs/If ever I cease to love . . .

May sheepheads grow on apple trees/If ever I cease to love.")

Carnival legend held, and still holds, that the twenty-two year old Grand Duke came to New Orleans in pursuit of Lydia Thompson, the musical actress who popularized the song, and whose acquaintance he had made months earlier in New York. But the newly enshrined lyric nonsense failed to rekindle Alexis's infatuation for Lydia; late on Mardi Gras night, he called instead upon her younger rival, Lotta Crabtree, with a bracelet of turquoise, pearls, and diamonds, and after a delay of several days joined the imperial fleet awaiting him in the Gulf of Mexico.

This first Rex parade not only revived the old Creole procession, it created enduring symbols and proclaimed royal trappings of Mardi Gras that were accepted and soon beloved by New Orleans—the King of the Carnival, *Boeuf Gras*, the Carnival colors, and the lilting anthem. The hurried preparations that marked the first appearance of Rex in 1872 did not characterize his reign. Superb organization shaped the decade that followed, as Rex added new rites and rituals to Carnival. Rex did not hold a ball in his first year, but on Mardi Gras night 1873, Exposition Hall was transformed into Carnival Palace; the invitations were in French. His Majesty entered with his royal court, and, to the strains of "If Ever I Cease to Love," marched twice around the ballroom floor in search of a queen. Rex himself chose Mrs. Walker Fearn, who, in her "second-best black dress" was crowned the first Queen of the Carnival.

The following year, the Rex organization was incorporated as the School of Design, and the royal coat of arms—a shield emblazoned with the Carnival colors and flanked by Jupiter and Hercules—soon distinguished the School's correspondence and proclamations. Rex also staged his first triumphal entry into the city in 1874. Beginning in the months before Mardi Gras, "Xariffa," the poet laureate, began to chronicle the progress of the king on his travels from the distant East as he returned to his Carnival Capital. These whimsical reports, along with sundry edicts, were featured in the daily press, and created widespread anticipation and enthusiasm; on the day before Mardi Gras, Rex arrived by steamer, and was greeted by a cheering multitude.

The Rex arrival unfolded at the Mississippi River, which was to New Orleans what the Adriatic was to Venice, the source of her wealth and greatness. Following a formal welcome by the mayor, the king and his courtiers were driven in carriages to the elegant St. Charles Hotel. One of Rex's edicts commanded all theaters to offer special presentations, without charge, to all of His Majesty's loyal subjects; this custom was honored for several years, and appreciative audiences hailed the king and his retinue as they made their way to each theater. During the parade on the next day, as he paused at a reviewing stand, Rex pointed his scepter toward debutante Margaret Maginnis, formally mentioned her name, and designated her Queen of the Carnival. From these beginnings, Rex's Monday arrivals, the Mardi Gras pageants, and the evening balls grew in splendor and fame.

The Rex "Reception Balls" were spectacular events, with thousands of invitations issued to a wide cross section of society, including many visitors to the city. The Rex membership did not mask, and there were no tableaux, but the throne and ballroom were always lavishly decorated. Guests in Carnival costumes were allowed during the first five years, but in 1878 Rex published the following instruction: "The Lord High Chamberlain desires it to be plainly understood that no gentleman will be admitted unless he is in full ball dress, and that ladies must come without bonnets." The first Queen of the Carnival had worn a bonnet to the ball; a decade later Her Majesty's jewels were a copy of Queen Victoria's. In 1885, the entire interior of the Carnival Palace was transformed into Sherwood Forest, using papier-mâché; no images of these early receptions have survived, but the invitations to them are tantalizing records of their brilliance.

Many of the Rex invitations and dance cards from the 1880s and 1890s were created in Paris by master lithographers such as Sicard, or the renowned J. Appel, whose firm designed posters for the Paris Opera; the invitations designed by New Orleans artists Charles Briton and Bror Anders Wikstrom were no less superb. Briton's design for the Rex ball of 1882 was in the form of a smiling, portly king wrapped in a purple velvet robe; as the two folds of the robe were opened, each became a multi-hued wing, and the jolly monarch was transformed into a butterfly king, a brilliant embodiment of Rex's theme that year, "The Pursuit of Pleasure." Wikstrom's design for the 1896 invitation for the subject "Heavenly Bodies" was a tour de force that incorporated the phases of the moon, hinged with a paste sapphire set in a metallic star, and rising above the midnight blue earth, which was dotted with a cascade of silver stars forming the date and the words "Rex, New Orleans, and LA." Wikstrom, a noted marine painter and former sailor, was clearly delighted with the Rex subject for 1897, "On the Water—Real and Fanciful." This fantastic invitation was a large die-cut Viking ship in the form of a highly carved dragon, decorated with eighteen lithographed shields depicting watery scenes and legendary vessels; the discs were layered in circles of three, and fastened with tiny golden crowns to both sides of the design.

Rex, more than any other Carnival society, greeted the twentieth century with an appetite for change. Beginning in 1900, Rex abandoned the elaborate die-cut invitations of old for engraved cards; dance cards remained die-cut and brightly colored, but they no longer reflected the subject of the parades. In 1901, Rex suddenly found the *Boeuf Gras* too barbaric for his pageant, and his procession, "Human Passions and Characteristics," rolled without the ancient symbol. Because of World War I, Carnival activities were canceled for 1918 and 1919, and when the King of the Carnival returned in 1920, he did so without his beloved Monday river pageant.

When the Great Depression began a decade later, with the collapse of the stock market on October 29, 1929, much of the work for the Carnival of 1930 had already been completed. But the economy of New Orleans, as everywhere else in the country, was soon devastated, and years of hardship and cutbacks followed. Elegance, mystery, beauty, and romance remained the fuel of Carnival balls and pageantry, but the Golden Age of Mardi Gras, the gilded era of fantastic productions and lavish expenditures begun sixty years earlier, drew to an emphatic close.

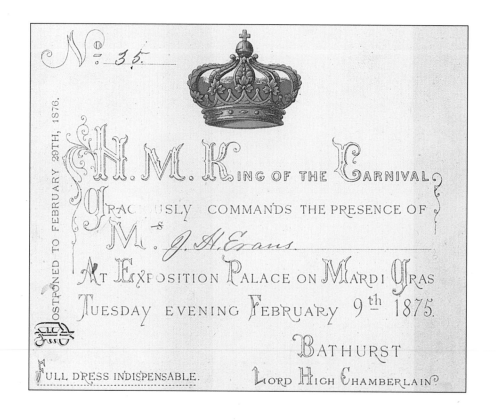

*Par ordre du Roi du Carnaval
Le Grand Chambellan
à l'honneur de prévenir
Melle C Morgan
qu'elle est invitée à passer la
Soirée au Palais de L'Exposition
le Mardi Gras, Vingt Cinq Février
1873, à 9 heures.*

On est prié de montrer cette carte en entrant.

Above: *Invitation to the first Rex Ball, 1873.*

Below: *Gentleman's admit card to the Rex Ball, 1875-1876. The Rex parade and ball of 1875 were canceled in reaction to Reconstruction tensions. Note the explanation on the left corner of this card: "Postponed until February 29, 1876."*

POSTPONED TO FEBRUARY 29TH, 1876.

N.⁰ 35.

H. M. KING OF THE CARNIVAL
GRACIOUSLY COMMANDS THE PRESENCE OF
Mr. J. A. Evans
AT EXPOSITION PALACE ON MARDI GRAS
TUESDAY EVENING FEBRUARY 9th 1875.
BATHURST
LORD HIGH CHAMBERLAIN

FULL DRESS INDISPENSABLE.

Invitation to the Rex Ball, 1875.

Invitation to the Rex Ball, 1877: "Military Progress of the World."

Envelope (top) and detail of invitation (bottom) to the Rex Ball, 1880: "The Four Elements."

Invitation (interior detail, opposite) *to the Rex Ball, 1882:*
"The Pursuit of Pleasure." Design by Charles Briton.

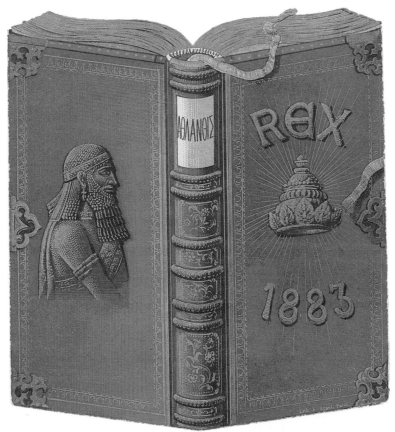

Opposite: *Invitation to the Rex Ball, 1881: "Arabian Nights Tales." Design by Charles Briton.*

Top: *Admit card to the Rex Ball, 1883: "Atlantis, the Antediluvian World." Lithography by F. Appel, Paris.*

Center: *Envelope for invitation to Rex Ball, 1883: "Atlantis, the Antediluvian World." Lithography by F. Appel, Paris.*

Bottom: *Admit card to the Rex Ball, 1884: "The Semitic Races." Lithography by F. Appel, Paris.*

Invitation (interior detail, opposite) *to the Rex Ball, 1884:*
"The Semitic Races." Lithography by F. Appel, Paris.

Invitation to the Rex Ball, 1885: "Ivanhoe."
Lithography by F. Appel, Paris.

Invitation to the Rex Ball, 1886: "The Triumph of Aurelian" and "Grand Historical Scenes."

Admit card to the Rex Ball, 1887: "Music and Drama." Lithography by Sicard, Paris.

Invitation to the Rex Ball, 1887: "Music and Drama." Lithography by Sicard, Paris.

Invitation to the Rex Ball, 1889: "Treasures of the Earth."
Each of the eight scalloped scenic panels folds into the center of
this glorious invitation.

Invitation to the Rex Ball, 1890: "Rulers of Ancient Times."

Rex 1891

Imperial Reception Febr. 10th.
Carnival Palace
New Orleans La.
By The King

Rex

Bathurst
Lord High Chamberlain

Invitation to the Rex Ball, 1892: "Symbolism of Colors." All twelve of
the die-cut lotus petals fold into the center of this work; six of them offer
scenes from the watercolor float plates. Design by Bror Anders
Wikstrom.

Opposite: Invitation to the Rex Ball, 1891: "Visions." Design by Bror
Anders Wikstrom.

Invitation to the Rex Ball, 1894: "Illustrations From Literature." Design by Bror Anders Wikstrom.

The phases of the moon
and a celestial cloud-bank are
affixed to this remarkable invitation with a metal clasp set with a
paste sapphire. Opposite, interior detail:
Showers of stars spell out the magical names of Rex
and New Orleans, reflecting the theme of the Rex pageant of
1896, "Heavenly Bodies." Design by Bror Anders Wikstrom.

Interior panel of Rex invitation, 1896: "Heavenly Bodies."
Design by Bror Anders Wikstrom.

Interior panel of Rex invitation, 1896: "Heavenly Bodies."
Design by Bror Anders Wikstrom.

Invitation to the Rex Ball, 1897: "On the Water—Real and Fanciful." Each side of this Viking ship was decorated with nine shields gathered in groups of three (see example below) and affixed to the vessel with metallic golden clasps. Design by Bror Anders Wikstrom.

Dance card for the Rex Ball, 1913: "Enchantments and Transformations."

Dance card for the Rex Ball, 1916: "Visions From the Poets."

Invitation to the Rex Ball, 1930: "The Jewels of Rex."

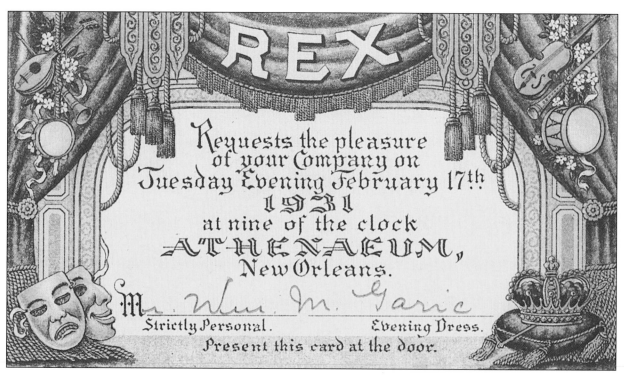

Invitation to the Rex Ball, 1931: "The Story of the Drama."

CHAPTER III

THE TABLEAUX SOCIETIES

Since the early days of colonial Louisiana, Creole society had celebrated Twelfth Night, the feast of Epiphany, with *Bals de Roi* (The King's Ball). These balls were given at plantations and homes for family and friends; the highlight was the cutting of the King Cake (*Gateau des Rois*), and the finder of the bean—"*la feve*"—in his or her cake became *Le Roi* or *La Reine de la Feve*, and would reign over the next ball, which they were to host. Thus a series of balls began each season and continued until the final great ball of Mardi Gras evening. These traditions were formalized with the organization and first appearance of the Twelfth Night Revelers, on January 6, 1870.

During their first six years, the ball of Twelfth Night Revelers was preceded by a pageant through the streets of New Orleans, with small floats, bands, torches, and a host of Revelers marching inside large papier-mâché forms. Following their last parade in 1876, Twelfth Night Revelers became the first Carnival society whose activities were limited to the staging of a tableaux ball, but it was the Twelfth Night ball of 1871 that inaugurated a custom that became one of the enduring and most emulated traditions of the festival—the selection of a queen. An enormous Twelfth Cake was cut, and its slices distributed to the young ladies by the Revelers; whoever found the gold bean (a bean-shaped locket) in her cake was named queen. At their first ball in 1870, court fools and jesters had made a clumsy show of serving cake on their spears, and the finder of the bean chose not to acknowledge her good fortune. However, the following year the Lord of Misrule knew which slice contained the bean, and when he saw the young lady receive it, strode to her, and before the assembled guests, crowned her with a wreath of oak leaves and proclaimed her "Queen of the Ball."

Twelfth Night Revelers survived several seasons of inactivity and reorganization during the 1880s, each time returning to open Carnival festivities on January 6. In the years of the *Belle Époque*, several new societies were created to satisfy the New Orleans passions for dance and masked balls—The Atlanteans (1891), Elves of Oberon (1895), Krewe of Nereus (1896), and the High Priests of Mithras (1897).

The great masquerade balls of earlier years were staged in the grand rooms of the St. Louis and St. Charles hotels, and public masked balls continued in theaters, ballrooms, and halls of numerous civic and social organizations. The tableaux ball of the krewes, which all came to be called "Carnival Balls," were presented on the elegant stages of the Varieties Theater, the Grand, or New Opera houses. After the Varieties and the Grand were destroyed by fire, almost all of the Carnival balls were staged at the New Opera, which after 1880 was known as the French Opera House. This beautiful Greek Revival theater, built in 1859, was designed by James Gallier, Jr., the younger of the famous father and son team of Irish architects. Writing thirty years later, in *Diary of an Impressionist*, Lafcadio Hearn remembered the great building:

> "The old French Opera House I have seen painted in a peculiarly pleasing hue, to which a summer sun would lend the mellowness of antique marble. It was a ripe-ivorine tint, with just the faintest conceivable flush of pink; it was a warm and human color—it was the color of Creole flesh!"

All the Carnival balls were similar in structure and ritual. A number of tableaux were performed, with beautifully scenic decors and fabulously costumed and masked krewes illustrating each year's theme. The last tableaux incorporated a throne setting, and the monarchs and court of the evening were presented with pomp and solemnity, to be greeted with the wonder and adulation of the entire assembly, krewe, and guests alike. The final tableaux was followed by a triumphant grand march of the entire court. Then came dancing, with the first quadrilles reserved for krewe members, followed by general dancing, which lasted until the early hours of the morning.

The royal courts were the central figures of the balls, but the extravagant tableaux were also designed to delight two thousand guests. The new societies of the 1890s turned for inspiration to themes long favored by Comus—mythology, literature, history, and nature—and while the processions rolled with their panoply of effects, the tableaux balls drew upon the stagecraft of the era, when theater and spectacle were often synonymous.

The first Atlantean ball paid tribute to their ruler, Poseidon, then reenacted "The Destruction of Atlantis." For their second production, the Atlanteans turned to Shakespeare and "*The Tempest,*" with tableaux depicting the shipwreck and Prospero's cave. *The Bird Wife*, one of the earliest Japanese tales to be translated by Lafcadio Hearn, was the subject of the 1893 ball; it was followed by an impressive series of themes which included: "The Ballet of the Seasons at Fontainbleau" (1894); "The Temple of Fame" (Alexander Pope) (1899); "The Last of the Incas" (1900); "Court of the Great Mogul, Shah Jehan" (1907); "The Realm of Precious Gems" (1903); and "The Starry Host" (1910).

The Elves of Oberon, the High Priests of Mithras, the Krewe of Nereus, and the Olympians transformed the stages of the French Opera House into a succession of fanciful kingdoms. Oberon's first ball featured two tableaux from "*A Midsummer Night's Dream.*" Subsequent efforts revealed a taste for whimsy: "A Rhineland Fancy" (1897); "The Rainbow" (1898); "The Christmas Tree" (1899); "Cupid on Vacation" (1902); "When Folly Rules" (1903); "Satan Dethroned" (1912); and "The Island of Dreams" (also by Hearn) (1901). Nereus, in his 1897 production of "Coral Groves and Grottoes," unleashed a huge kraken that was one hundred feet long, supported by fifteen men, and belched fire as it writhed across the floor of underwater caverns. The first two Mithras balls turned to Persian themes—"Prince Ahmed and the Fairy Banou" (1897) and "Mithras, God of the Sun" (1898). Fire broke out in the stage decorations of the latter, and while the flames were readily extinguished, many of the guests fled in panic. But dozens of others remained, and danced for hours around the pool of water the stage had become.

The papier-mâché decors and painted backdrops for these tableaux balls were executed by the reigning scenic artists of New Orleans. Georges Soulie, the city's finest sculptor in papier-mâché and builder of the most prominent pageants, maintained a studio in the French Opera House. Scenic painting for the stages of numerous theaters, for Bidwell's Academy of Music, the Grand Opera, and the French Opera House was provided by Harry H. Dressel, Robert De Lapouyade, and the members of three families active for decades—the Bagnettos, the Cox Brothers, and the Deutschmann Brothers. With the exception of early Twelfth Night invitations, most of which can be attributed to Charles Briton, and a handful of Atlantean designs that were clearly the work of Jennie Wilde, the artists who designed the invitations to the tableaux balls have remained anonymous.

With the entry of the United States into World War I, all Carnival balls and parades were canceled. In 1919, none of the society krewes appeared with parades or balls, but a number of masquerade balls were held, and Mardi Gras counted many maskers. All through the year 1919, preparations for Mardi Gras of 1920 were underway when, only weeks before Twelfth Night and the opening of the Carnival season, the French Opera House was destroyed by fire. At about 3:00 A.M. on the morning of December 4 the fire broke out, most likely in the Café de l'Opera, and within hours the Palace of Carnival was reduced to rubble. The French Ambassador to the United States wired his condolence to the French Consul General in New Orleans, deploring the loss of this symbol of Creole culture. On the following day, Lyle Saxon wrote in the *The Times Picayune*:

"Gone, all gone. The curtain has fallen for the last time upon 'Les Huguenots,' long a favorite of the New Orleans public. The opera house has gone in a blaze of horror and glory. There is a pall over the city; eyes are filled with tears and hearts are heavy. Old memories, tucked away in the dusty cobwebs of forgotten years, have come out like ghosts to dance in the last, ghastly Walpurgis ballet of flame . . . The heart of the old French Quarter has stopped beating."

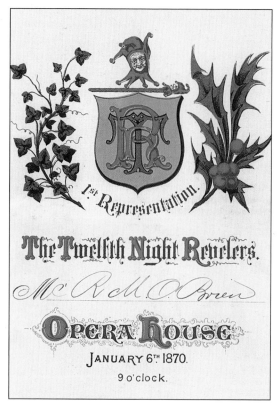

Invitation to the first ball of the Twelfth Night Revelers,
1870: "A Twelfth Night Revel."

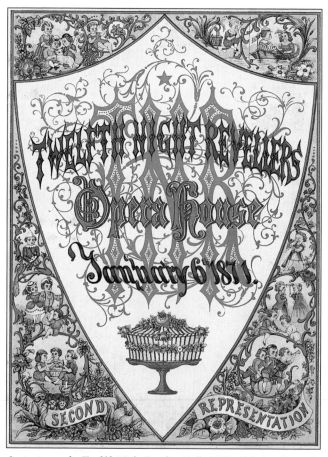

Invitation to the Twelfth Night Revelers Ball, 1871: "Mother Goose."

Invitation (above) and admit card (below) *for the Twelfth Night Revelers Ball, 1872: "English Humor." Designs by Charles Briton.*

Invitations for the Twelfth Night Revelers Ball of 1875 (above) had been delivered, but the parade and ball for that January 6th, "The March of Ages," were
both canceled due to lingering tensions of Reconstruction. Invitations for 1876
(below) offered a graphic explanation of the Revelers failure to appear—the
Lord of Misrule was shown surrounded by bayonets. Designs by Charles Briton.

TABLEAU I.

This engraving is one of the few surviving tableau scenes of early Carnival balls.
The first tableau of "A Twelfth Night Revel" presented the court of the Lord of
Misrule in 1878. Design by Charles Briton.

Invitation (right) and dance card (below) for the Twelfth Night Revelers Ball, 1884: "The Kingdom of Flowers." Designs by Charles Briton. "January 7 Last evening to the fete of the Twelfth Night Revelers. Ballroom very handsome with giant palmettoes, flowers and hundreds of caged birds. With a wild burst of music, the masked Revelers stalked in, marched round the hall, at a signal broke ranks, each captured a partner and the ball opened with the 'Maskers Quadrille.' My Reveler wore a terrific devil mask which did not hide his merry blue eyes. We all trooped to the end of the room, where on a raised dais stood a mammoth cake made up of many little boxes filled with goodies; one held beside a ring. The lucky girl who got it became the queen of the ball. Home very late, escorted by some of the Revelers, who left us at our door, and went off singing a pretty Creole song, 'Adieu, ma Belle.'" Maud Howe Elliot, Three Generations.

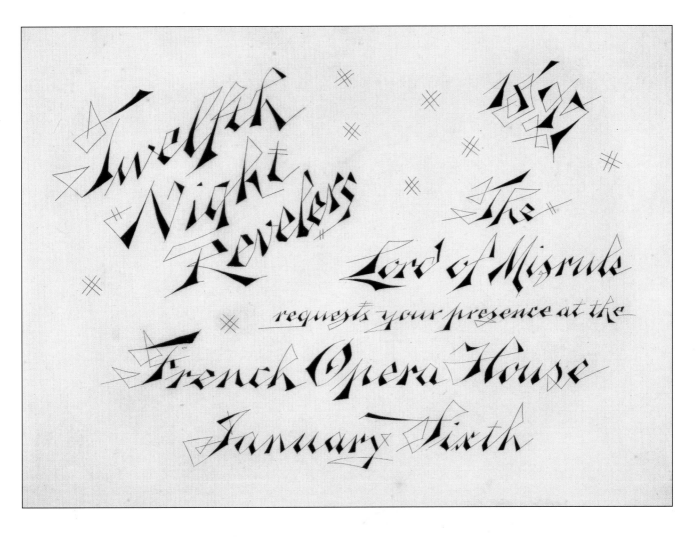

*Deeply engraved invitation (above) and multi-hued dance cards (below)
for the Twelfth Night Revelers Ball, 1897: "The Chrysanthemum."*

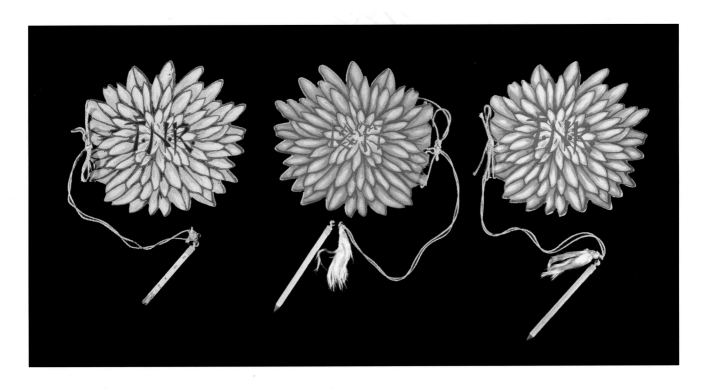

Dance card for the Twelfth Night Revelers Ball, 1899: "The Realm of the Butterflies."

Dance card for the Twelfth Night Revelers Ball, 1911: "The Battle of the Flowers."

Right: *Dance card for the Twelfth Night Revelers Ball, 1913: "The Origin and Quaint Customs of Twelfth Night."*

Below: *Program for the Twelfth Night Revelers Ball, 1938, "A Reminiscence of Lafcadio Hearn."*

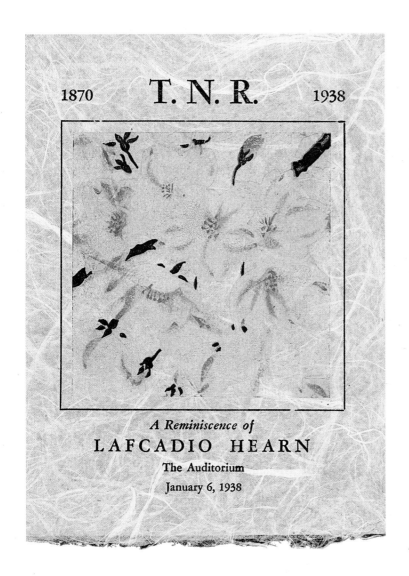

1870   **T. N. R.**   1938

A Reminiscence of
LAFCADIO HEARN
The Auditorium
January 6, 1938

*Invitation (above) and admit card (below) to the first ball of
The Atlanteans, 1891: "Destruction of Atlantis."*

Invitation to the Atlanteans Ball, 1907: "Court of the Great Mogul."

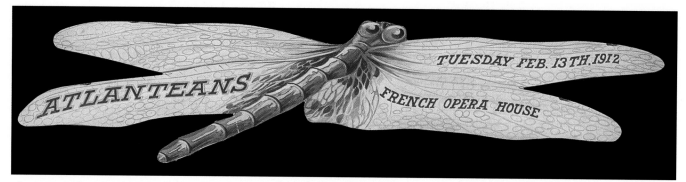

Invitation to the Atlanteans Ball, 1912: "Poseidon Visits Mars." Design by Jennie Wilde.

Invitation to the Atlanteans Ball, 1908: "The Realm of Hyperion." Design by Jennie Wilde.

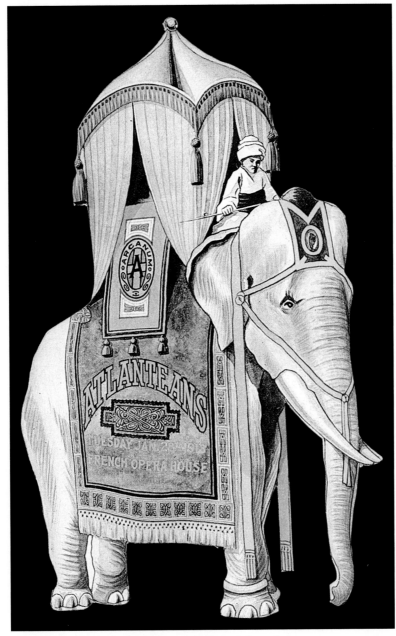

Invitation to the Atlanteans Ball, 1913: "The Country Circus."

Invitation to the Atlanteans Ball, 1911: "Undine." Design by Jennie Wilde.

Dance card for the Elves of Oberon Ball, 1903, "When Folly Rules."

Above: *Dance card for the Elves of Oberon Ball, 1912: "Birth of the Carnival."*

Right: *Dance card for the Elves of Oberon Ball, 1900: "Chance."*

The Tableaux Societies .... 89 ....

Invitation to the Krewe of Nereus Ball, 1897:
"Coral Groves and Grottoes."

Dance card for the Krewe of Nereus Ball, 1897: "Coral Groves and Grottoes."

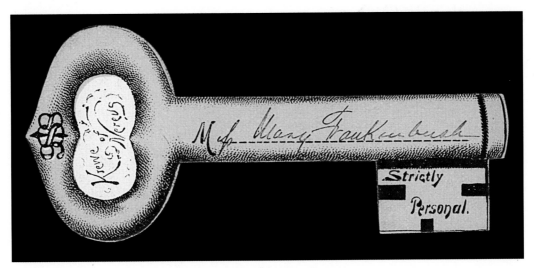

Lady's admit card for Krewe of Nereus Ball, 1898: "The Inferno."

Invitation and dance card (opposite) for the
Krewe of Nereus Ball, 1898: "The Inferno."

Dance card (above) and invitation (below) to the Krewe of Nereus Ball,
1900: "The Christian Era."

Top: *Lady's admit card to Krewe of Nereus Ball, 1902: "The Fountain of Youth."*

Bottom: *Dance card for the High Priests of Mithras Ball, 1910: "The Tale of the Ninth Statue."*

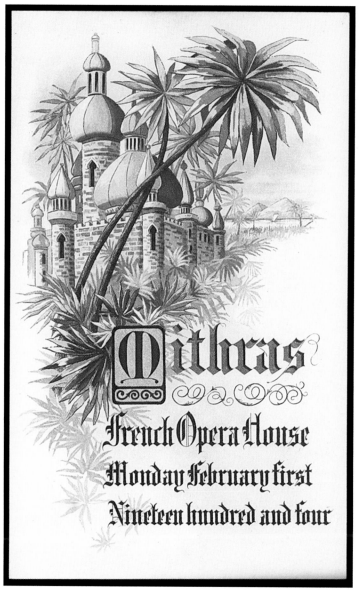

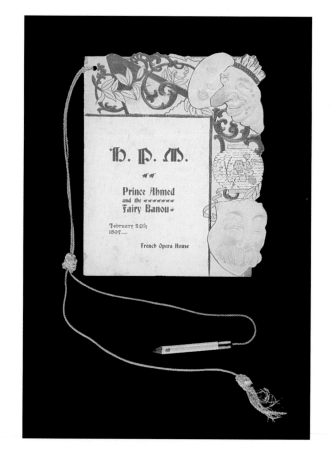

Invitation to the High Priests of Mithras Ball, 1904: "The Story of Shah Nemah."

Right: *Dance card for the High Priests of Mithras Ball, 1897: "Prince Ahmed and the Fairy Banou."*

Invitation to the High Priests of Mithras Ball, 1922: "The Search of Prince Satni After the Magic Book." Design by Anne McKinne Robertson.

Above: *Dance card for the Olympians Ball, 1913: "A Starry Fantasy."*

Right: *Dance card for the Olympians Ball, 1917: "Revel of the Pierrots."*

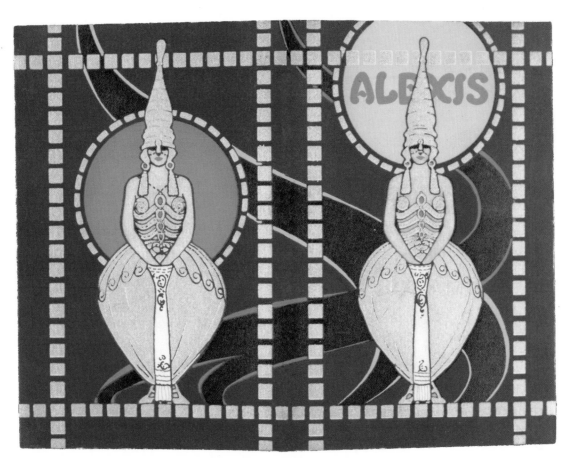

Dance card for the Alexis Ball, 1924: "A Winter Palace Ball."

Dance card for The Mystic Club Ball, 1924: "A Mandarin's Joy Ride."

Program for The Mystic Club Ball, 1927: "Monsieur Beaucaire."

CHAPTER IV

KNIGHTS OF MOMUS

On the morning of December 30, 1872, the editorial page of the *The Picayune* alerted New Orleanians to the first appearance of a new Carnival krewe:

"By a mysterious and symbolic missive dropped into the Sanctum of the Picayune, and requiring the services of an interpreter to decipher the cabalistic signs, we learn that the Knights of Momus propose appearing on the evening of New Year's Eve."

The New Year's Eve edition the next day carried an announcement signed "Momus," which set forth rules for the gala ball to be held that evening at the French Opera House. One of the rules, printed in bold type, read: "ALL TICKETS BEING COMPLIMENTARY ARE PERSONAL AND CANNOT BE TRANSFERRED."

Invitations to this first ball reflected the knightly theme, *"The Talisman,"* and bore the elaborate cipher "K. O. M." To the left an aged Father Time was pictured with his scythe, amid barren winter branches; to the right floated a cherubic Infant Year, with his cornucopia of blossoms and butterflies; and painted on a profusion of winding ribbons was the name "Knights of Momus" and the most

delightfully apropos motto in all of Carnival: *"DUM VIVIMUS VIVAMUS,"* "While We Live, Let Us Live!"

In Greek mythology, Momus, the god of laughter, mockery, and raillery, was the son of the goddess Night and an unknown sire. No one on Olympus was secure from the barbs of Momus. He criticized Zeus for not placing the bull's horns on his shoulders, where they could do more harm; he chided Hephaestus, the Olympian foundryman, for not forming man with a window in his breast so that his real feelings might always be seen; and when Poseidon, Athena, and Hephaestus appealed to the son of Night to judge their godly merits, he dismissed all three of them as good-for-nothings. Small wonder then, that Momus and his sister Eris, goddess of discord and strife, were rarely invited to the feasts and fetes of the gods. But among the Carnival Gods of New Orleans, Momus was second only to Comús in age or glory, and for generations his Thursday night procession marked the beginning of the season's public festivities.

The second Momus pageant, and his last on a New Year's Eve, was the 1873 production of "The Coming Races." No coherent descriptions of the

ST. JOHN THE BAPTIST PARISH LIBRARY
1334 WEST AIRLINE HIGHWAY
LaPLACE, LOUISIANA 70068

procession or the two tableaux given at the Varieties Theater have survived, and the ball invitation is both strange and nonsensical. It depicted a host of animal mutants and hybrid creatures, and several denizens of this beastiary bore the torsos of renowned naturalists, among them John James Audubon and Charles Darwin. Unlike "The Missing Links," the Comus masterwork of the preceding Carnival, "The Coming Races" was more devoted to nonsense than to satire, and much of its humor has been lost.

This was not the case four years later, in 1877, when Momus presented the most vitriolic satire in Carnival history, "Hades: A Dream of Momus." In the waning days of Reconstruction, the son of Night vented his Olympian spleen with a procession of devils and demons who were the papier-mâché twins of officials in the Republican administration of President Ulysses S. Grant. The engraved ball invitation carried no hint of the hell to be unleashed, but the fabled street pageant and ball tableaux were designed by the remarkable Charles Briton. The handful of surviving watercolor float designs for Momus in the 1870s and early 1880s, as well as the lithographed Carnival editions of parades (lithographed sheets that depicted the parade floats), and newspaper illustrations of ball tableaux, were all the work of Briton. His hand can be seen in a few of the Momus invitations, but almost all of them were designed by anonymous artists employed by lithographic firms in Paris or New Orleans.

The political satire of Momus would lie dormant for a century, but wit and comic flair continued to distinguish many of his presentations. For his subject in 1878, Momus chose "The Realms of Fancy," and in 1880, "A Dream of Fair Women," with his Knights masked and costumed to represent, among others, Dido, Delilah, Cleopatra, Joan of Arc, Mary Stuart, and Elizabeth I. Momus, however, was not always comic; like Comus, he also turned to lofty themes, as he did in 1882 with "The Ramayana," one of India's two great literary and religious epics, and in 1883 with "The Moors in Spain." The stunning invitation for "The Ramayana" was a large gilded paper octagon, with sixteen die-cut petals that opened to form a perfect lotus; the dance card

was in the form of a small white lotus, and the admit card was a scalloped, die-cut, and richly-veined lotus leaf.

Momus staged neither parade nor ball in 1886 or 1888, and when he returned to the Carnival of 1889, his festivities were limited to balls. In 1896, the Knights of Momus presented their greatest tableaux ball, "A Comic History of Rome," a miniature pageant on the stage of the French Opera House. The dance card was in the form of a die-cut she-wolf dressed in Roman robes, and holding the apprehensive infant founders. The staging was ingenious. The curtain rose upon a scene of Canal Street, with the Pickwick and Boston Clubs in the background, their balconies crowded with eager beauties. These ladies, as well as the restless throng awaiting the parade and every other character in the show, were all members of the Knights of Momus, costumed for their parts. There were policemen and torch-bearers, bands, horses, and the captain and his aides, followed by eighteen diminutive floats, executed in papier-mâché with beautiful detail. *The Picayune* reported:

> "The miniature pageant was over an hour passing the Pickwick Club, and on the march all the incidents usually attending Carnival pageants, even to a break-down, were noticed."

Momus celebrated the end of the nineteenth century with a production of "Cinderella, or the Little Glass Slipper." *The Picayune* reported the general laughter and hilarity that filled the French Opera House as Cinderella's two large "stepsisters" attempted to squeeze their feet into the storied slipper. In 1900, after a hiatus of eleven years, Momus returned with a brilliant street pageant on his traditional Thursday night, "Legends From the Court of King Arthur." Jennie Wilde designed the Momus floats from 1900 until her death in 1913; the dance cards for 1908 and 1909 can also be attributed to Wilde, but for his ball invitations Momus retained the format of engraved cards.

Following the end of World War I and the burning of the French Opera House, Momus refrained from parading until 1923, and during this period moved his ball to the new stages of the Athenaeum. Comparison to the glories of the Opera were painful, but while the brilliance of the Carnival balls was diminished, the high spirits of Mardi Gras and the old krewes proved irrepressible. In celebration of that spirit, the Momus ball of 1921 presented "The Battle of Don Carnival and Lady Lent." Small booklets recounted the annual battle, as told by Juan Ruiz, the arch-priest of Hita, Spain; illustrations for this little book were the first Carnival work of Louis Andrews Fischer, then completing her studies at Newcomb Art School. The beautifully written tale, augmented by tableaux, began with the formal challenge of Lady Lent to Don Carnival:

"From my Lady Lent, Justice of the Sea-Watch, Officer of Souls that are to be Saved, to you, Lickerish Carnival: I command you to stop your gluttonish eating and drinking. . . . Within seven days you and your company must meet me on the battlefield, for I am determined to fight you without mercy until Holy Saturday, and either imprisoned or dead, you will not be able to escape me!"

"Sir Carnival called his army together, his foot soldiers, the Chickens and Partridges, Rabbits, and Fat Geese; then came the archers, Lady Hung Beef, Mutton, Chops, Fresh Pork, and Whole Hams. Then came the Fresh Cheese, to spur on the chattering Ruddy Wines . . . then came the Great Feast.

"And Sir Carnival, with his jugglers and jesters, and his ensign and his large army, laughed and shouted death to Lady Lent and drank deep and ate and danced until late, and feel asleep at midnight.

"Lady Lent fell upon them with her army of brave soldiers, the White-necked Leek, the Salted Sardine, the Dog-fish and the Cuttle-fish . . . and from Valencia came the Eels . . . the Oysters fought the Rabbits, the Rough Crabs struggled with the Hares . . . From one party and another great blows were given; the valleys were full of scales and blood. The troops of the sea marched on together and fell on Sir Carnival. Then did Lady Lent hold Don Carnival captive for full forty days of doleful penance and many prayers and confessions did he have to make, with doleful sighs and shedding of many tears. And

a very slim diet did he have to eat. . . . And during all of that time he was ordered to go to the cemeteries, to visit the churches, to pray in his psalm book, to attend holy mass in order to get relief from his sins and benefit from the stern discipline of Lady Lent. Don Carnival grew very pale and very thin, and very good, indeed, while Lady Lent, having won the fight, went all around the world, cleaning up all manner of dirt, scrubbing away sins and making all do penance. But while Lady Lent was busy, and as the days went by, Don Carnival grew stronger and began to set up in bed, and to plot for his escape from prison.

"So when Palm Sunday came Don Carnival pretended to be very contrite and went to mass, but while his guard Fasting was praying, Don Carnival escaped and found good lodging in the Butcher's Shop. And in his escape he was aided by Don Breakfast, a clever wight; by Fat Lunch, and by the greatest of all rogues, Sir Love, who brought his bow and arrows with him. From the Butcher Shop, Sir Carnival sent out a message of defiance to Lady Lent, and from this headquarters he sent out messages of greeting to his loyal subjects, who quickly rallied to his aid. Dame Lent ignored this challenge. She announced that she had made a vow to go on a Pilgrimage to Jerusalem, and also vowed that she would return: 'You all who hope to keep me captive cannot hold me; for an old fish is not caught in all the nets.'

"Then did Sir Carnival hold sway. The Sun has risen. It is Easter Eve, and Don Carnival reigns as Emperor over all his subjects. From his golden throne in his golden tent, with bright pennants flying their colors, he reigns. From all the villages came the pretty maids and lads, dancing and singing, in a procession, and with them all the birds and beasts of the fields. Sir Carnival is Emperor over all, and to his court in the period of gaiety came all of the gay, pretty months of the year, with singing. Sir Thursday, Lord Momus, the God of Laughter, at this season also holds his court and helps, while I write, to show you the pictures which emblazon this merry old tale, written in the year of our Lord 1300."

Invitation to the first ball of the Knights of Momus, 1872: "The Talisman."

Gentleman's admit card to the Knights of Momus Ball, 1873: "The Coming Races."

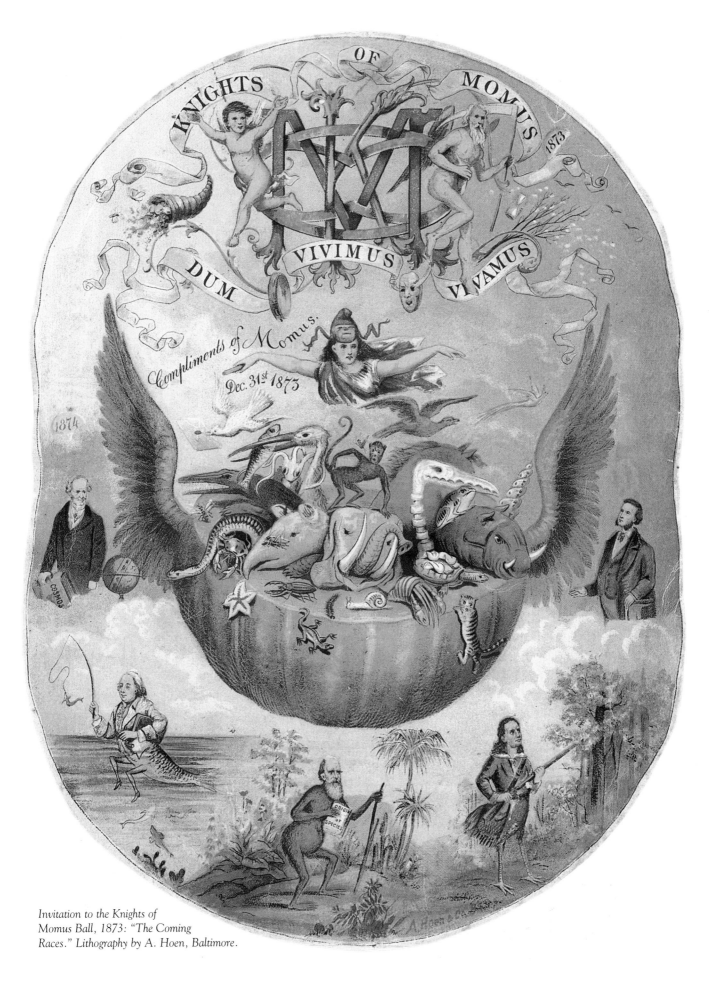

Invitation to the Knights of Momus Ball, 1873: "The Coming Races." Lithography by A. Hoen, Baltimore.

Exterior of invitation to the Knights of Momus Ball, 1878: "The Realms of Fancy." Note the bizarre vignette, upper right, with alligator, rotund fairy, and pelican with breasts. Design by Charles Briton, lithography by Gonthier-Dreyfus, Paris.

Interior of invitation to the Knights of Momus Ball, 1878: "The Realms of Fancy." Design by Charles Briton, lithography by Gonthier-Dreyfus, Paris.

This suite of Aesthetic Movement wonders—the white lotus dance card (above), the richly-veined lotus leaf admit card (left), and the octagonal lotus invitation (opposite)—was created by Charles Briton for the Momus Ball of 1882, "The Ramayana." In the course of this remarkable Carnival season, Briton also designed the first pageant and ball for the Krewe of Proteus, the parade and Butterfly King ball invitation for Rex, and the Silver Anniversay procession and ball for the Mistick Krewe of Comus.

Invitation to the Knights of Momus Ball, 1883: "The Moors in Spain." Design by Charles Briton. This ball marked the first of two occasions when Momus paraded and held court on Mardi Gras night.

Above: *Dance card for the Knights of Momus Ball, 1884: "The Passions."*
Design by Charles Briton.

Below: *Admit card and invitation (following page) to the Knights of Momus*
Ball, 1885: "The Legends Beautiful."

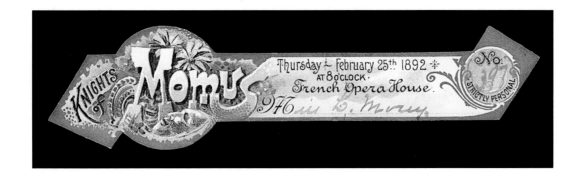

Admit card (above) and invitation (below) to the Knights of Momus Ball, 1892: "Aladdin or The Wonderful Lamp."

Dance card for the Knights of Momus Ball, 1894: "The Fairies and The Fiddler."

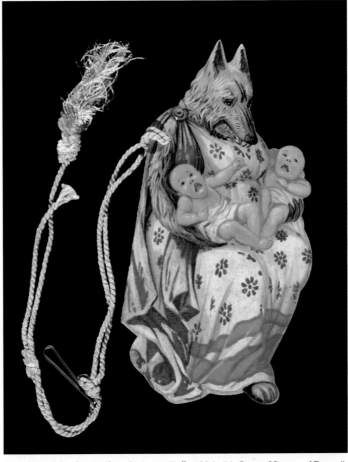

Dance card for the Knights of Momus Ball, 1896: "A Comic History of Rome."

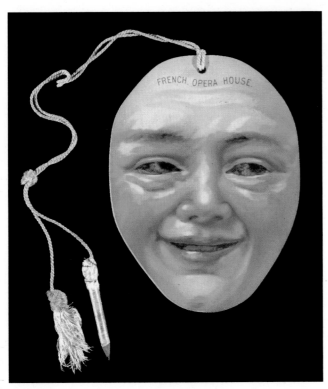

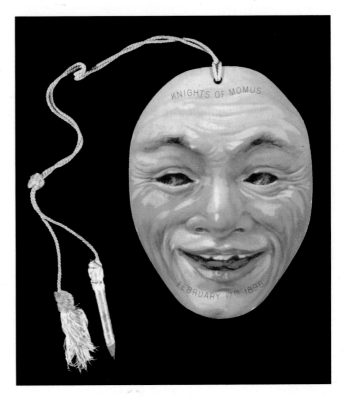

Front and back of dance card in the form of a classic wax mask, for the Knights of Momus Ball, 1898: "Bal Masque."

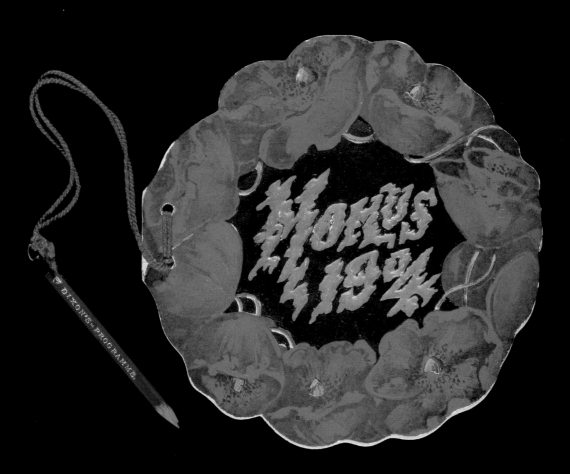

Above: *Dance card for the Knights of Momus Ball, 1904: "Visions of the World's Vanities."*

Below: *Dance card for the Knights of Momus Ball, 1908: "Aesop's Fables."*

Above: *Dance card for the Knights of Momus Ball, 1913: "Above the Clouds."*

Below: *Dance card for the Knight of Momus Ball, 1912 (Fortieth Anniversary): "Chronicles of Momus."*

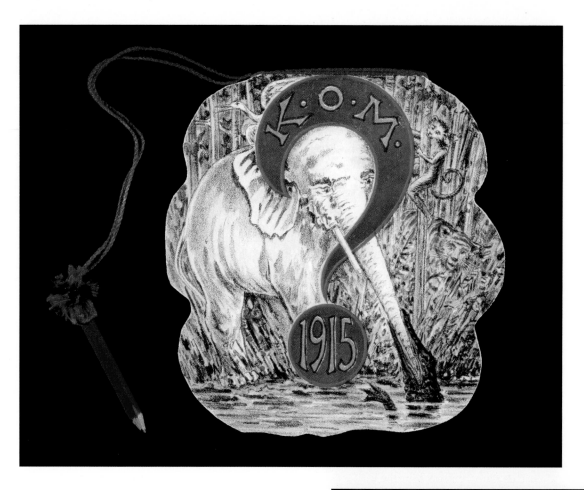

Above: *Dance card for the Knights of Momus Ball, 1915: "Tales of the How and Why."*

Below: *The fabulous Carnival career of Louis Andrews Fischer began with the illustration of this medieval Spanish tale for the Knights of Momus Ball, 1921: "The Battle of Don Carnival and Lady Lent."*

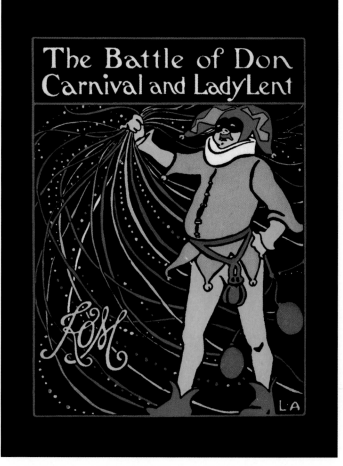

CHAPTER V

KREWE OF PROTEUS

On the night before Mardi Gras in 1882, the Krewe of Proteus made its astonishing debut. Because waiting lists for membership in Comus and Momus had grown so long, a new society was created by a group of young men "largely from the New Orleans Cotton Exchange." Proteus was an inspired addition to the Carnival firmament; this herdsman of the sea deified the bonds between New Orleans and the waters, and to a pantheon of sorcery and mischief he brought the ineffable gift of changing form at will. *The Daily Picayune* recounted the first appearance:

"Long ago, in the age of myth and fable, when the gods lived on the earth, there dwelt on the island Pharos, Proteus, the Prophetic Old Man of the Sea, son of Neptune, whose flocks, the seals, he tended. At midday the ancient god rose from the ocean and slept in the shade of the rocks with the monsters of the deep lying around him. Any one wishing to learn the future from him was obliged to catch hold of him at that time. As soon as he was seized, he assumed every possible shape in order to escape the necessity of prophesying; but whenever he saws that his endeavors were of no avail, he resumed his usual form and told the truth. He then returned into the sea . . . The god has at length awakened from his slumber of centuries in the Nile, and Proteus and his krewe have come out of the ancient land, with the old gods of Egypt—behold them, in the Alexandria of modern times, the great city on the banks of the New World's Nile."

"Ancient Egyptian Theology" was composed of seventeen papier-mâché floats, recreations of temples, tombs, palaces, and pleasure gardens, sacred animals, and resurrection. Proteus appeared through the mist and smoke and glare of torches "riding upon the back of a huge flying Dolphin that seemed just springing from the crest of the mighty wave that surged beneath. In his right hand he held his scepter, while in his left were gathered the reins of his water courser. His flashing armor gave back the light from a thousand glittering pints, and the shining scales of his Dolphin shed flashed like a million diamonds. Its enormous wings reflected the colors of the rainbow. Before him, on the back of finny monsters, rode his heralds, a Triton and a sea nymph, blowing upon huge horns of sea shell, while about them in the tumbling waters swam hurrying fish of every description." This wondrous scene of Proteus enthroned was repeated on invitations to the first ball.

Proteus was the first Carnival krewe with a sizable Creole membership, and a Creole captain. And as Comus had called attention to his Anglo-Saxon origins with his production of "The English Holidays" in 1859, Proteus, in his second year, chose to illustrate "The History of France." The Proteus invitations for 1883 were die-cut in the form of fleurs-de-lys, and depicted scenes such as Hesus, the Druid God of War, in his chariot, the Baptism of Clovis, and LaSalle taking possession of Louisiana. Dance cards for the evening were die-cut flags attached to small wooden standards; one side was painted with the golden fleur-de-lys of the Bourbons, the other with the tricolor of Republican France.

Charles Briton designed the first three Proteus pageants, and while the first two invitations were clearly his work, 1884's *Aeneid* invitation came from another source.

Briton's successor with Proteus was the mysterious Carlotta Bonnecaze, the first woman (Jennie Wilde's career began five years later), as well as the first Creole, to design floats and costumes for the societies. Many of the Proteus invitations were printed in Paris by premier lithographers, and some of them were designed by French artists who have remained anonymous. But several others, notably "Myths and Worships of the Chinese" in 1885 and "Visions of Other Worlds" in 1886, were based on the remarkable Bonnecaze float designs for those parades. The Chinese invitation depicted Proteus in the guise of Tien-Dze, the son of heaven, astride the Fong-Hoang, or Phoenix; beneath him were panels illustrating the Creation, the birth of Confucius, and the Chinese Hells—one of fire, one of ice. Invitations to "Visions of Other Worlds" were large cards illustrated with bizarre images of spectral water gods and a host of denizens from the moon, comets, and other planets, some of them riding atop a large salamander.

Invitations of the late 1880s and early 1890s were designed to surpass all other Proteus efforts. In 1888, "Legends of the Middle Ages" invitations were folded into the die-cut form of a large silver chalice. The angular chalice was richly chased with small geometric patterns and human figures that, upon closer inspection, revealed themselves to be vignettes that depicted scenes and motifs from the previous six years. As the multiple sections of the chalice were unfolded, one entered that year's triumph, with scenes such as the Nibelung hoard, Hagen in the griffin's nest, and Percival crowned king of the grail.

"The Hindoo Heavens" of 1889 was equally brilliant and intricate; a series of eight highly ornamental, die-cut frames (each of them printed with scenes front and back) opened out from a central octagonal panel, unveiling a multiplicity of Indian gods and goddesses, demons, angels, and Paradise.

Two of the most elaborate Proteus invitations are not pictured in this book—"Tales of the Genii" (1891), which opened out like a storybook pop-up, depicted a large Arabian palace, garden, and carpeted stairway (only fragments of this work are to be found today) and "A Dream of the Vegetable Kingdom" (1892), which likewise moved into three dimensions, and opened to form a free-standing basket of flowers and fruit, but the design ingenuity was exhausted in the mechanics, and the invitation lacked either the zany wit or striking color of the float designs. The following year, Proteus returned to form with a beautiful ten-pointed star illustrating "The Kalevala." In 1894, the Sea God presented "Shah Nameh, the Epic of the Kings," and his invitations were large Persian fans, set into elegant handles, illuminated with colorful miniature paintings, and decorated with a braid of embossed gold paper; dance cards were in the form of elaborate Persian quivers, and embossed with the golden profile of Shah Nameh.

With the coming of the twentieth century, Proteus and Comus were the only two Carnival krewes whose invitations and dance cards continued the lavish traditions of the Gilded Age. In this decade, when Jennie Wilde was producing her Art Nouveau masterworks for Comus, Bror Anders Wikstrom, the dean of New Orleans Carnival artists, began to design the Proteus pageants.

"Orlando Furioso," in 1897, was the first Proteus parade that can be attributed to Wikstrom, who also designed the invitation, a die-cut shield that pictured Orlando subduing the monstrous orc. The invitations continued to reflect the subject of the processions, and while most of them incorporated something of Wikstrom's float designs, only a handful of them appear to have been designed by him.

"Al Kyris the Magnificent," in 1901, continued Carnival's fascination with Arabian themes: the exterior panels, die-cut in the form of butterfly wings, were framed with the flowing robes of the storied potentate; the interior panels, airily painted in pale greens and white, offered a dreamy feast of Wikstrom's favorite eastern architecture—pavilions, minarets, gardens, and kiosks. Among the verses illustrated in the 1905 production of "The Rubáiyát," was "The Cup of Life," which also appeared as the central design motif of the invitation. Proteus celebrated his silver anniversary in 1906 with a unique invitation: large booklets, bound with silver cord, opened upon detailed representations of all twenty-four preceding invitations; the highly embossed cover was decorated with an exuberant border of cloud-like acanthus leaves and silver bells, and "Krewe of Proteus 1906."

Wikstrom's successor, or his string of successors, remain unknown; from 1908 until the interruption occasioned by the onset of World War I, the Proteus invitations seem to have come from a different hand each year. And while the papier-mâché apparitions of the pageants went largely unchanged during the second decade of the twentieth century, the ball invitations had begun to shed their luster. The palpable sense of design that infused the invitations of the Golden Age was strangely diffused in the efforts for "Astrology" (1910), "The Last Days of Pompeii" (1911), "Adventures of Telemachus" (1913), and "Gerusalemme Liberata" (1914), and the brilliant hues and dramatic contrasts of earlier lithography were seldom found in the anemic, monochromatic palettes of that decade's modernism. The successive catastrophes of World War I and destruction of the French Opera House compelled Proteus to withdraw from Carnival for five years, and when he returned in 1922 with "Romance of the Rose," his medieval pageant was designed by the brilliant young Louis Andrews Fischer. However, invitations to this first ball at the Athenaeum assumed the bland form that would follow for twenty years with only minor alteration. A slender white, horizontal card was lettered in black, "Krewe of Proteus," together with the ball location and date; small vignettes, also printed in black, and hinting at the parade subject, appeared on invitations of the 1920s, but this decorative excess was deleted after 1930, an early casualty of the Great Depression. The fabulous designs and artistry of the old invitations were relegated to the realm of things that were.

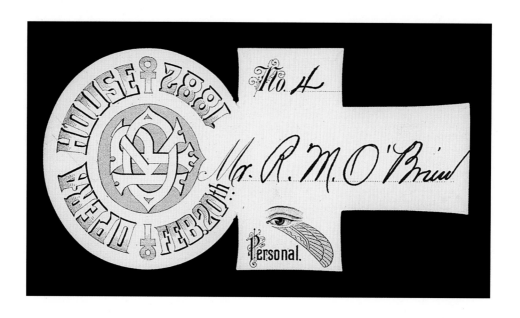

Admit card (top) *and invitation* (bottom) *to the first Krewe of Proteus Ball, 1882: "Ancient Egyptian Theology." Proteus appears on his float from the inaugural pageant. Designs by Charles Briton.*

Dance card (above) and invitation (right) for the Krewe of Proteus Ball, 1883: "The History of France." Designs by Charles Briton.

Invitation to the Krewe of Proteus Ball,
1884: "The Aeneid."

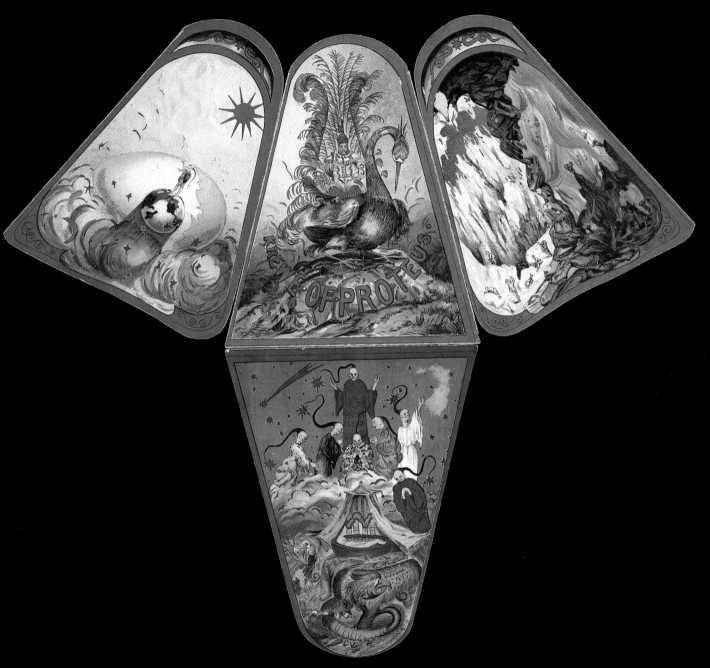

Invitation to the Krewe of Proteus Ball,
1885: "Myths and Worships of the
Chinese." Design by Carlotta Bonnecaze.

Dance card for the Krewe of Proteus Ball, 1888: "Legends of the Middle Ages." Lithography by F. Appel, Paris.

Opposite: Dance card (top) and invitation (bottom) for the Krewe of Proteus Ball, 1886: "Visions of Other Worlds." Designs by Carlotta Bonnecaze.

Invitation to the Krewe of Proteus Ball, 1890: "Elfland." Lithography by F. Appel, Paris.

Opposite: *Invitation to the Krewe of Proteus Ball, 1888: "Legends of the Middle Ages." Lithography by F. Appel, Paris.*

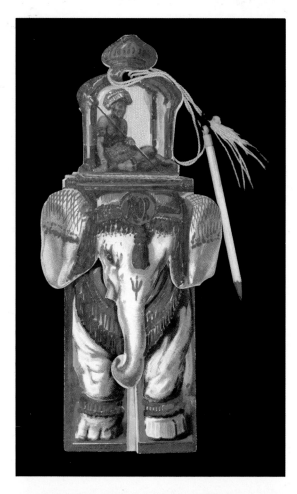

The dance card (left), lady's admit card (below), and invitation (opposite) to the Krewe of Proteus Ball, 1889: "The Hindoo Heavens."

Left: *Dance card for the Krewe of Proteus Ball, 1891: "Tales of the Genii."*

Below: *Dance card for the Krewe of Proteus Ball, 1892: "A Dream of the Vegetable Kingdom."*

Opposite: *Invitation to the Krewe of Proteus Ball, 1894: "Shah Nameh, the Epic of the Kings."*

Lady's admit card (above) *and dance card* (below) *for the Krewe of Proteus Ball, 1894: "Shah Nameh, the Epic of the Kings."*

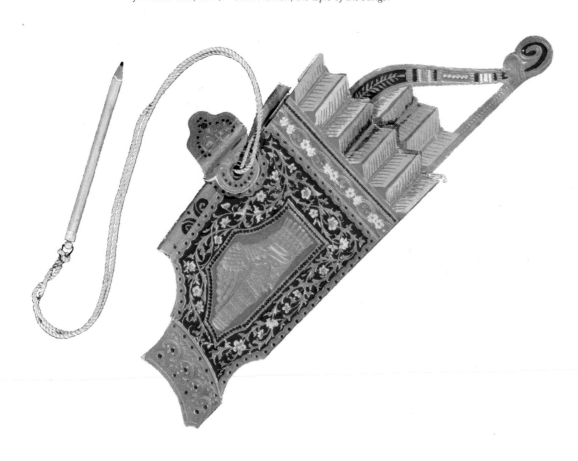

Invitation to the Krewe of Proteus Ball, 1897: "Orlando Furioso." Design by Bror Anders Wikstrom.

Invitation to the Krewe of Proteus Ball, 1899: "E Pluribus Unum." Design by
Bror Anders Wikstrom.

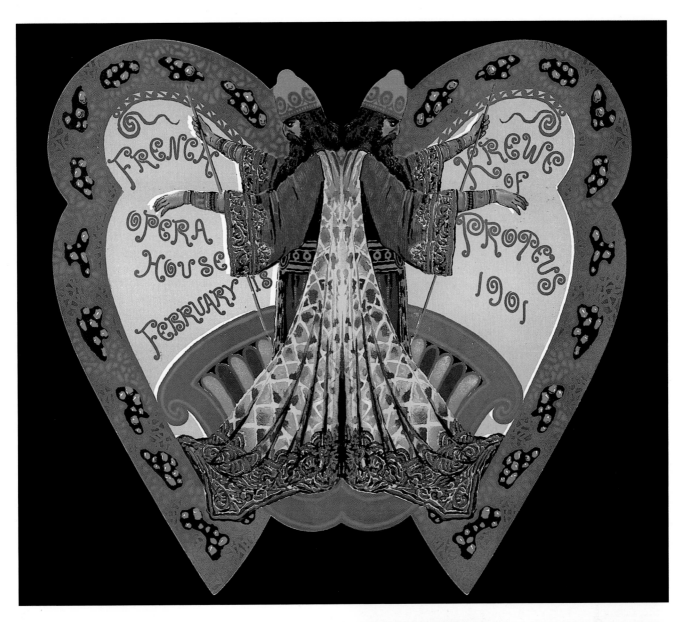

Above: *Invitation to the Krewe of Proteus Ball, 1901: "Al Kyris the Magnificent." Design by Bror Anders Wikstrom.*

Right: *Dance card for the Krewe of Proteus Ball, 1902: "Flora's Feast."*

*Dance card (above) and admit cards (below) for the
Krewe of Proteus Ball, 1903, "Cleopatra."*

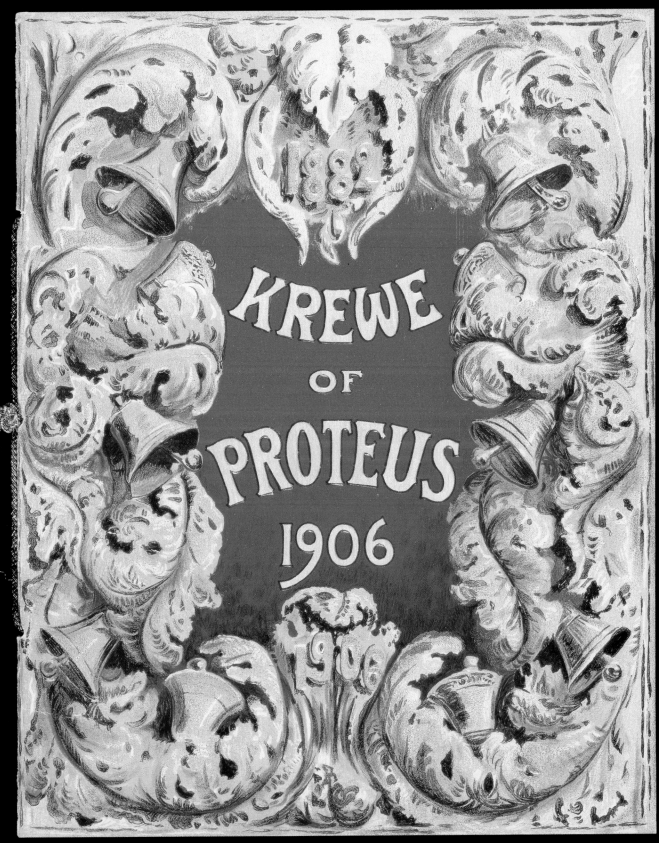

Program for the Silver Anniversary Ball of the Krewe of Proteus, 1906:
"The Inspirations of Proteus." Design by Bror Anders Wikstrom.

Left: *Dance card for the Krewe of Proteus Ball, 1908: "The Light of Asia."*

Below: *Detail of invitation to the Krewe of Proteus Ball, 1907: "The Queen of the Serpents."*

*Invitation to the Krewe of Proteus Ball, 1908: "The
Light of Asia."*

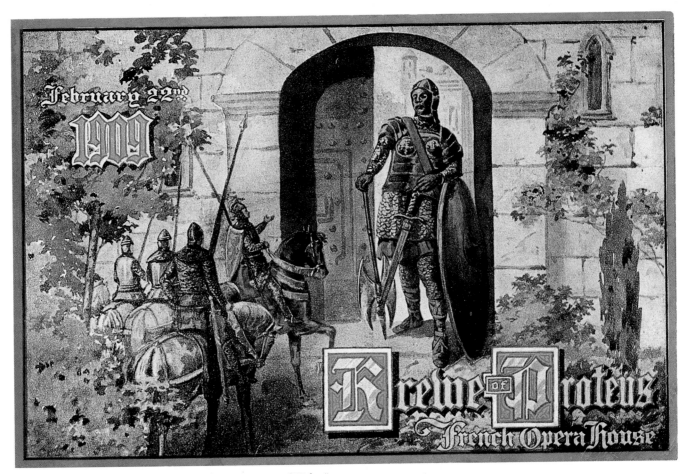

Invitation to the Krewe of Proteus Ball, 1909: "Romances of Wales."

Opposite: *A scene from the Krewe of Proteus Ball at the French Opera House, 1907.*

Invitation to the Krewe of Proteus Ball, 1913: "Adventures of Telemachus."

CHAPTER VI

SOCIÉTÉS PERDUES

To comprehend the magnitude of the New Orleans devotion to the pleasures of Carnival and tableaux balls of the "Golden Age," one must survey the large number of societies that blossomed, flourished, and then vanished. A few of these krewes—Disciples of Thespis, Phunny Phorty Phellows, Independent Order of the Moon, Mistick Merrie Bellions, and Mystic Krewe of Druids—presented humorous and satirical parades that were as beloved as the lofty artistic processions of Comus, Rex, Momus, and Proteus. But a larger number of these lost societies limited their activities to balls—at the French Opera House, Odd Fellows Hall, Werlein Hall, St. Charles Theater, Grunewald Hall, and the Athenaeum: The Growlers, Harmony Club, Les Mysterieuses, Consus, Young Men's Hebrew Association, The Falstaffians, The Mystic Maids, The Mittens, Amphictyons, Krewe of Yami, Krewe of Nippon, The Follies, and Carnival Revelers.

The press, which had reported lists of committeemen and details of tableaux balls for decades, could not get enough. In 1870, the first mention of ladies at the Comus ball only dared print their initials—Miss Maggie D., Miss Josephine S.; by the early 1880s, names of ladies and descriptions of their gowns appeared, and lists of ladies called out to dance soon followed. From Twelfth Night to Ash Wednesday, portraits of all the Carnival courts, half-tone drawings framed in scrolls and ovals, graced the front pages of newspapers. There was no Twelfth Night Revelers ball in 1882, and The Growlers appeared with their first and only ball. The society column of *The Daily Picayune* ran this note:

> "My Dear Old Lady: Of Course I was at the Growlers' Ball. Their entertainments are always delightful, but last night they really excelled themselves. The floral decorations were simply superb. There were so many beautiful dresses worn by beautiful women that for my life I couldn't describe one. I shut my eyes and try to think, and I see only a mass of beauty and loveliness, bright eyes and diamonds, til I am dazzled. Your own, Bee."

Sir John Falstaff, the celebrated character in Shakespeare's *Henry IV* and *Merrie Wives of Windsor* was the reigning spirit of The Falstaffians, as well as the inspiration of their first three balls—"Falstaff's Dream in Windsor Forest," "Sir John's Army," and "The Court of Falstaff." A feature of their balls, all of them staged at the French Opera House, was the intricate, soldier-like drill of the cast. With their inaugural ball in 1900, Falstaffians became the first krewe born in the twentieth century, and the group flourished for sixteen years, but for reasons unknown they failed to appear in 1917, and following World War I, their revels were never revived.

The first female krewe, Les Mysterieuses, appeared only twice at the French Opera House, in the leap years of 1896 and 1900, with brilliant evenings of role-reversals and wry detail. The parterre, usually graced with lovely women, was filled with several hundred gentlemen, waiting to be called out to dance with their masked partners. The king and his dukes, many of them leading members of Rex and Comus, occupied a proscenium box and were costumed in white satin directoire finery and powdered wigs. The queen and her cast were attired in directoire gowns sparkling with jewels, and they alone were masked. Jeweled fobs were bestowed upon the men as favors. The 1900 ball repeated the reversals of masking and call-outs; there were four queens—Brunhilde, Juliet, Semiramis, and Pocahontas—and each of them, with her attendants, descended into the sea of white ties to select a king. The stage was set in gold and white, with motifs of the crimson poppy, the emblem of silence. "It was good for the men," wrote *The Picayune* society editor, "Now they'd get to see how it felt for a girl to sit and wait to be called-out to dance."

Among the many societies of Carnival's Elysium, none was more widely loved or more greatly mourned than the Phunny Phorty Phellows. They first appeared in 1878, marching behind the Rex parade as the Rex Fire Company No. 40, a parody of the fire company parades so popular across the country. The Phellows had no king or throne car; they had The Boss, who rode a horse at the front of the parade. For eight years the Phunny Phorty followed Rex, with small floats that satirized the known worlds of politics, government, temperance, fashion, and celebrity. No ball was staged in their first two years, but beginning in 1880, the P. P. P.

held forth on Mardi Gras evenings. The comedic style and general hilarity of their parade was carried into their revels at Odd Fellows Hall, and the grand march was led by Brother Jonathan and the Goddess of Liberty.

Guests of the Phunny Phorty on Mardi Gras night of 1883 were summoned to the elegant St. Charles Theater, where the Phellows performed four tableaux selected from "Visions of the Stage." The remarkable invitation to this ball was created at the height of the Aesthetic Movement, whose high priest, Oscar Wilde, had been a recent visitor to New Orleans; the P. P. P. took aim at the flamboyant playwright with "An Ass-thetic Bray," and its donkey-headed dandy holding a sunflower. The Phunny Phorty returned to the St. Charles in 1884 with "*As You Like It*," but their parade the following year was less ambitious than usual, there was no ball, and the acclaimed society appeared to be gone forever. However, eleven years later, the P. P. P. revived their activities for three seasons, and from 1896 through 1898 presented parades and balls; guests were now invited to the French Opera House, and the ball was no longer held on Mardi Gras night, but on the preceding Friday. One sub-heading for the extensive *Picayune* coverage of the ball proclaimed it "A Foretaste of Their Mardi Gras Display," while another announced "The Crowning of a Chosen Queen of Beauty." The Boss and his Phellows now had a Queen and a court of maids, but their devotion to hilarity and nonsense was undiminished:

"All was decorous as the Queen and her maids approached. The bears curbed their ursine instincts, the Indians whooped not, and never a hoot escaped the owl. First walked Boss, in his princely robes, carrying a scepter that cost $40,000,000 in Samarcand and that sparkled with gems big enough to throw at a cat.... At last the moment came for the beginning of the tableaux, and amid a flourish of sounds from the orchestra the big curtain rolled softly up and settled with a comfortable thud against the ceiling. An electric button touching off a cannon could not have brought more instantaneous applause than arose from the audience at the first sight of the scene on the stage. It was realized at a flash that here was a genuine Carnival ball. The maskers were arranged in silent groups within a great court, the studio of

'Boss,' Chief of the Phunny Phorty Phellows. Every variety of costume, laughable, ridiculous, grotesque, was to be seen. Here was a fool in tights and tunic, cap and bells upon his head and a long nose and painted face. There was a bear, next to him a monkey, beyond a devil, and scattered round were to be seen Persians, Indians, Ladies of the Harem, Baboons, Fiends, and Donkeys.

"In the midst of this strange assembly which stood as if frozen, satirizing the recent tableaux of another Carnival organization which represented statuary [Oberon, "Visions in Marble"], stood the Royal Head of the P. P. P., 'Boss,' attended by his immediate retainers, Kickapoo, Donkey, and Owl. Slowly and solemnly the royal body moved until they reached the front of the stage, when Boss, producing an enormous Bologna sausage, brought it down with a wack upon the head of the nearest masker, the mystic signal which commanded the crew to awake from their statuesque poses. At the same moment a huge angel with muscular arms and lumpy legs, who had stood with mock devotion on top of a mammoth beer barrel, leaped high into the air and, fluttering his wings, descended fifteen feet to the floor, giving vent to a stentorian crow. These formalities through with, the maskers became animated and leaped round the stage with an activity strangely out of keeping with their previous silence and dignity. The Fools mouthed out nameless sounds, the monkeys brayed, the Indians war-whooped, and the Fiends and Devils raised a pandemonium of outlandish sounds. In the midst of this wild and picturesque scene, the curtain rolled softly down."

Consus brought the first of his spectacular productions to the French Opera House in 1897, launching a brief, ten-year reign of displays never surpassed in lavishness, invention, or detail. In 1898, Consus presented "The Meeting of King Henry VIII of England and King Francis I of France on the Field of the Cloth of Gold." *The Picayune* described the incredible scene:

"It is probable that glass had never before been used on so lavish a scale for the purpose of the decorator. The pattern on either side was of blue, amber, and opal glass, set alternately, the top and bases handsomely inlaid after a lotus leaf pattern. The semi-circle was composed of beveled plate glass . . . frosted, set in a diamond pattern, the intersections marked by imported cut-glass jewels. The front of each of the lower galleries, all the way to the horseshoe, was draped in cloth of gold. High in the center of the theater's dome was a golden spider-web, from which long filaments reached the galleries. The paradis was decorated in sky-blue silks, studded with silver fleur-de-lys, supported by silver headed spears."

In 1900, Consus presented "The House Boat on the Styx." The cast entered to the dirge of Chopin's Funeral March, and proceeded to a banquet hall with jewel-encrusted walls. The following year they chose "Shakespeare and His Creations," the only Carnival ball whose sets and decorations came wholly from nature—a forest of flowers, trees, moss, and palms. The next year boasted splendid recreations of eleventh-century Spanish costumes; the invitations were in Latin. At his final ball in 1906, Consus transported his guests to "The Land of Frontinback and Upindown," where his ingenious design populated the stage with reversals of nature. Forests and fields grew downward behind the proscenium arch, clouds and sky were underfoot. The men and women of Frontinback were also reversed in their movements, walking and dancing backward; to achieve these effects, Consus used double masks for his cast—the face on the mask covered the back of the wearer's head, while the back of the mask's head concealed the face of the krewe member.

Costumes lent the same illusion, buttoning over false fronts, and generously padded to mimic anatomical curves. As the tableaus were performed, the effects were stunningly impressive and supremely original; it seemed that Consus had added another triumph to his Carnival glory. But his cleverness had overlooked one thing—the appearance his krewe would present to their partners when they danced. Ladies found their partners' backs facing them, an unintended discourtesy that was all an illusion; but this illusion was so well-crafted that many of the ladies were deeply offended, and a flood of resignations quickly reduced the famous society to a memory.

The fancy dress and masquerade of the Well-Known Gentlemen and the C.C.C. Club predated Storyville; they were held on the Saturday before Mardi Gras and on Mardi Gras night, when the district's elite flocked uptown to the revels at Odd Fellows Hall.

Above: *Invitation to the Ball of the Well-Known Gentlemen, 1895.*

Right: *Invitation to the Ball of the C.C.C. Club, 1894.*

Dance card for the Les Mysterieuses Ball, 1900: "The Four Types of Fair Women."

Dance card for the Falstaffians Ball, 1911: "A Legend of the North."

Dance card for the Falstaffians Ball, 1903: "Hiawatha."

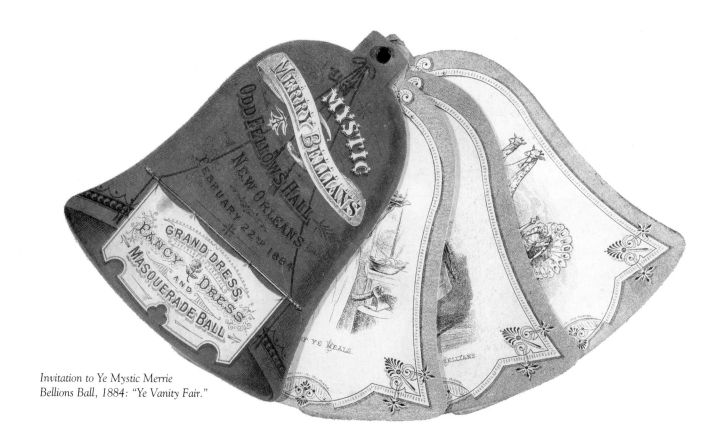

Invitation to Ye Mystic Merrie Bellions Ball, 1884: "Ye Vanity Fair."

Gentleman's admit card to the Phunny Phorty Phellows Ball, 1881: "Fair Women."

*Invitation (above) and dance card (left) for the Phunny Phorty
Phellows Ball, 1897: "Songs That Never Die."*

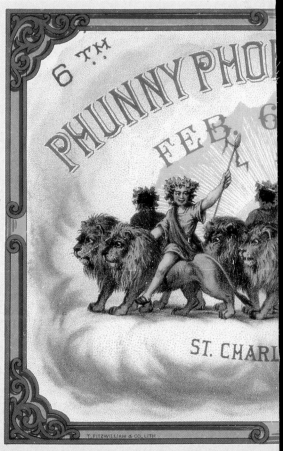

Invitation to the Phunny Phorty Phellows Ball, 1883: "Visions of the Stage." Design by Daniel Anton Buechner.

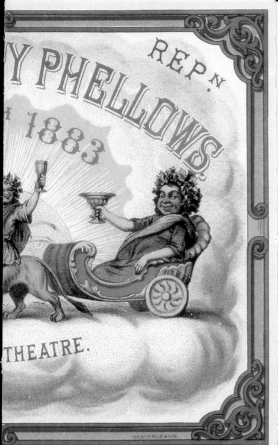

REP.N

1883

Y PHELLOWS

THEATRE.

NEW ORLEANS.

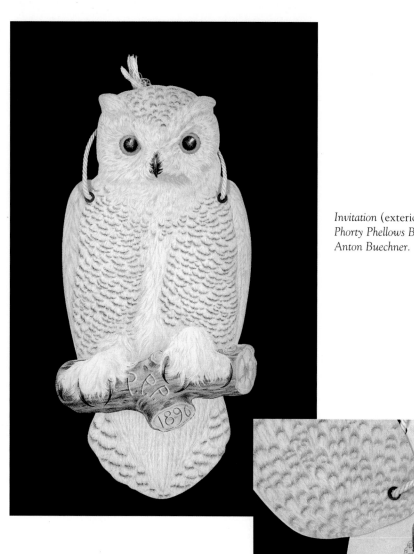

Invitation (exterior, left and interior detail, below) *to the Phunny Phorty Phellows Ball, 1896: "Phads and Phancies." Design by Daniel Anton Buechner.*

DE PAR LA VOLONTÉ DE
SA MAIESTÉ
FRANÇOIS ROY de FRANCE

Vous estes enjoinct d'auoir à paroistre
au Palais du Théatre de l'Opéra François
le vingt-huitiesme de Ianvier, MDCCCXCVIII,
à huit heures avec tous autres Seigneurs,
Gentilshommes, Dames et Damoiselles de
la Cour à effect d'assister aux Tournois,
Carrousels, Ioustes et Festins Royaux.

MARÉSCHAL DE FLORANGE
Maistre de la Maison de Consus.

Invitation to the Consus Ball, 1897: "The Meeting of King Henry VIII of England and King Francis I of France on the Field of the Cloth of Gold."

Above: *Dance card for the first Consus Ball, 1897: "Sherwood."*

Below: *Dance card for the Consus Ball, 1898: "The Meeting of King Henry VIII of England and King Francis I of France on the Field of the Cloth of Gold."*

Above: *Dance card for the Consus Ball, 1901: "Shakespeare and His Creations."*

Below: *Dance card for the last Consus Ball, 1906: "The Land of Frontinback and Upindown."*

INDEX

ACKNOWLEDGMENTS

I would first like to acknowledge the importance of Special Collections, Tulane University, to this project. The great majority of the material pictured in this book is housed there, and I am indebted to Dr. Wilbur Meneray, director of Special Collections, for his cooperation. For their kind and endless assistance, I would also like to thank the Collection staff members: Mary LeBlanc, Leon Miller, Courtney Page, Carol Hampshire, Kenneth Owen, Ann Case, Dr. Joan Caldwell, and Dr. Robert Sherer.

I would like to thank James F. Sefcik, director of the Louisiana State Museum, and Shannon Glasheen, acting registrar, for permission to use the Storyville invitations. Rene Vicedomini was a cheerful guide through hundreds of scans and downloads at Orleans Colour. I would like to acknowledge Owen Murphy's photography, and Fred Kahn's photography and Stephanie Cruppi's assistance at Colorpix. John Kelly's research assistance was invaluable, as was Jon Newlin's work on the index. I would also like to thank Arthur Hardy, Sidney Hebert, and Millard W. Morrison for their generosity with their collections.

At Pelican Publishing, I would like to acknowledge the enthusiasm of Dr. Milburn Calhoun for the series of Mardi Gras Treasures. It has also been a pleasure to work with production designer Tracey Clements, editors Nina Kooij and Winter C. Randall, and with typesetter Gwynn Harris.

And finally, I would like to thank my sister, Elaine Schindler Whitaker, for all of her patient help through the long hot summer of 1999.

New Orleans
April 2000

PICTURE CREDITS

Special Collections, Tulane University—page(s) 1, 2, 5, 6, 16, 17, 20, 21, 24-25, 26, 27, 28 (top), 31 (bottom), 37 (top), 38, 40 (top), 41 (top), 42, 46, 47, 48, 49, 52, 53, 56, 57, 59, 60-61, 62, 63, 64-65, 66, 70, 71, 72, 76, 77, 78, 79, 80 (bottom), 81, 82, 83, 84, 85, 86, 87, 88, 89 (bottom), 90, 91 (bottom), 92, 93, 94, 95, 96, 97, 98, 99 (bottom), 100, 104, 105, 108, 109, 110, 111, 113 (top), 114, 115 (bottom), 116, 117, 118, 122, 123, 124, 126 (top), 127, 128, 130 (bottom), 132 (bottom), 133, 134 (top), 135, 136, 137 (top), 138 (bottom), 140 (top), 141, 144, 149 (top), 150 (bottom), 151 (bottom), 155, 156, 157

Louisiana State Museum—page 148

Collection of Henri Schindler—page(s) 3, 12, 22-23, 28 (bottom), 29, 30, 31 (top), 32-33, 34-35, 36, 37 (bottom), 39, 40 (bottom), 41 (bottom), 50-51, 54-55, 58, 67, 68, 69, 89 (top), 91 (top), 99 (top), 112, 113 (bottom), 125, 126 (bottom), 129, 130 (top), 131, 132 (top), 134 (bottom), 137 (bottom), 138 (top), 139, 140 (bottom), 143, 149 (bottom), 150 (top), 151 (top), 154

Collection of Sidney E. Hebert—page(s) 19, 25 (bottom), 80, 106, 107, 142, 152-153

Collection of Millard W. Morrison—page 115 (top)

Collection of Arthur Hardy—page 18

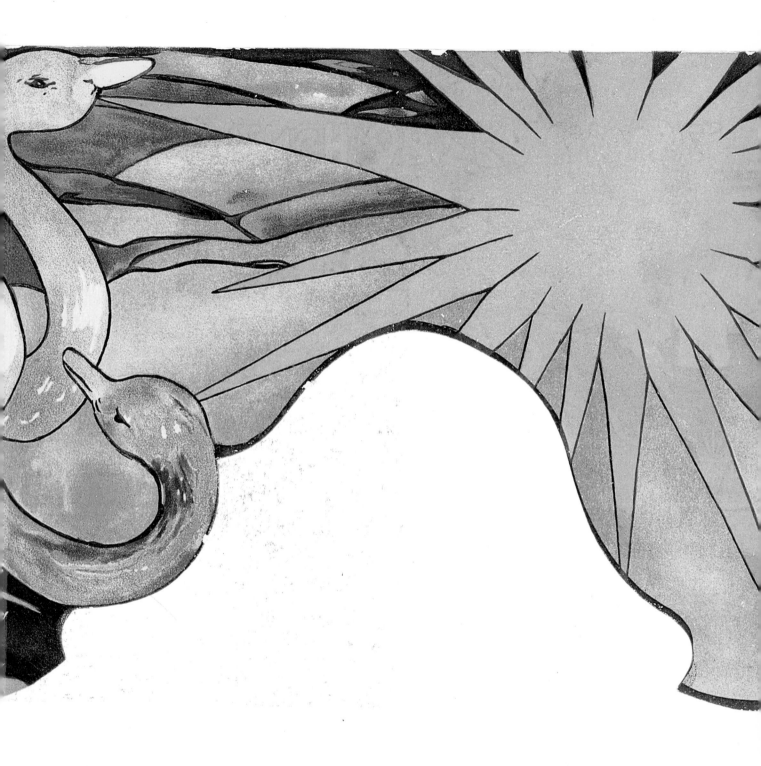